A Trip to
COLOMBIA

A TRIP TO COLOMBIA

HIGHLIGHTS OF ITS

SPANISH COLONIAL HERITAGE

Mark J. Curran

Order this book online at www.trafford.com
or email orders@trafford.com

Most Trafford titles are also available at major online book retailers.

Printed in the United States of America.

ISBN: 978-1-4669-7911-6 (sc)
ISBN: 978-1-4669-7910-9 (e)

Trafford rev. 02/12/2013

 www.trafford.com

North America & international
toll-free: 1 888 232 4444 (USA & Canada)
phone: 250 383 6864 ♦ fax: 812 355 4082

Dedicated to My Best Friend and Wife Keah, A Courageous Traveling Companion

Part Two in the Series: Stories I Told My Students

Table of Contents

PART III. BOGOTÁ AND BEYOND: TRIP TO THE NORTH AND HISTORIC BOYACÁ STATE

PART IV. CARTAGENA DE INDIAS

PART V. EPILOGUE TO COLOMBIA:
LA ISLA SAN ANDRÉS, MICROCOSM OF THE CARIBBEAN

LIST OF ILLUSTRATIONS

PREFACE

This book is a continuation in the series, "Stories I Told My Students." These "stories" however are a departure from the area of my main research interest: Brazil, its literature and its folk-popular literature, the "literatura de cordel." Colombia is a story born of necessity and enthusiasm: at Arizona State University and my post in the Department of Foreign Languages, a labor I enjoyed for 34 years full-time and 9 years part-time in early retirement, I would ask for and then "inherit" the senior level course SPA 472 Spanish American Civilization. The graduate professors in Spanish were not interested in the course, I surmise mainly because teaching the course would not lead to scholarly publications in literature or literary theory, and it truly took a "jack of all trades" to do the job well. It turned out to be my cup of tea due to both academic preparation (my Ph.D. minor in Latin American Studies had at least introduced me to similar material) and more importantly, love and curiosity of Latin America.

Furthermore, teaching the course forced me to expand my horizons in reading, preparation and travel the next thirty years. I found the endeavor altogether pleasant and rewarding, if not in publications (Brazil would take care of that), certainly in increasing my own knowledge and departing it to the students. I would always insist on teaching a split schedule at ASU each semester—two courses in Spanish and one in Portuguese—the latter really a matter of practicality with the far smaller enrollment in Portuguese Language and Literature. In this endeavor for SPA 472, however, months and years of study, teaching and travel would not only open the country of Colombia to me, but then the Pre-Colombian civilizations of Mesoamerica and the parts of Mexico, Guatemala and Honduras associated with them. And much later, there was more intense study and travel in Spain and Portugal, for indeed an introduction to Latin American Civilization had to begin with its roots. But all the latter is another story to be told later in the series.

The issue at present is Colombia. This country may be one of the most beautiful, varied and interesting countries of Latin America, even though its Pre-Colombian vestiges are "minor" compared to the Incas or the Mayas, or perhaps for a better word, "different." What it did have, and what I badly needed to know about was Colombia's rich colonial art and architecture and its major role in the development of Independence in South America. In the former, Colombia was rich in religious, military and residential architecture and arts. In the latter, its role for all of South America cannot be disputed. The country certainly ranks just below Mexico and Peru in its heritage and contribution to Spanish American Civilization. These attributes and interests will become evident in the narration.

The account is based on an intense period of travel, study and living in Colombia on a sabbatical leave from ASU in 1975. As I look back on the notes from that time, there as usual is some naiveté, but one of my mantras in class was, "You have to start somewhere." The trip was made easier by some wonderful hosts, Mr. and Mrs. Emery, Lorentz and Elaine, and their son James who really sparked the idea after earning an A in the Spanish American Civilization class at ASU the preceding year to the sabbatical. I think Jim thought I was leaving out an important chapter in the big story of Latin America. They were our guides, companions and friends. Shortly after the trip Mr. Emery was killed in a crash in the high Andes on the same roads we braved and careened around on in buses just a few short months earlier. He was not only a gentleman, a good and brave man, but enormously giving in sharing his wealth of knowledge of Colombia. And I owe a major debt to Jim, a fine student and friend. He would help set the itinerary, discover the travel tips and help us from getting mugged in the Colombian bus stations. It is to be noted that Colombia was still relatively safe for the traveler in 1975; the horrible days of guerrilla warfare, drugs and violence were to come later. But oh those pickpockets!

And a final introductory note: my young wife Keah would be my traveling companion and enthusiastic tourist at my side. She had taken the "cram" course in Spanish with me during evening classes at ASU in preparation for the trip, and although her spoken Spanish was minimal, she had a terrific "ear" and more than once told me what in the heck people were saying!

The narration is comprised, as I shall repeat later, in two segments: the serious search for the contributions of Colombia in the aforesaid arts and architectural heritage, and the experience of travel and tourism. The two shall be blended and shall reflect upon each other, a good thing I think.

INTRODUCTION

As mentioned in the preface to this book, the purpose of this trip was to go to a country that truly has maintained the colonial heritage of Spain in Latin America. I picked Colombia for several reasons: first, because to this point earthquakes had destroyed only part of the legacy, as opposed to a place like Guatemala which has been decimated since the sixteenth century; secondly, because we had heard of its beauty, and lastly, because of a close friend, a former student living in Bogotá, Jim Emery of ASU days. The trip came at the half way point of a sabbatical semester. In Tempe I wrote the Jorge Amado monograph until late February; then we left for two full months in Colombia. And at that time in 1975 it had been thus far the most productive and enjoyable sabbatical of all. The worst, by the way, was in 1982 when I stayed home the entire time to write the manuscript for a long book on Rodolfo Coelho Cavalcante, an important Brazilian "cordelian" poet, writing in our travel trailer at the side of our house in Tempe. Academically, the book on Rodolfo turned out well, but sitting in the trailer writing eight hours each day was decidedly less exciting than Colombia, but that is another story.

PART I. FIRST TRAVELS IN COLOMBIA

THE FLIGHT TO COLOMBIA

The trip took place at the height of Marriage Encounter days. Keah and I had helped give these "marriage enrichment" weekends for Catholics, so there was a large support community in Tempe and Phoenix, and we had emotional ties to many, many people. It was difficult to leave, but they helped us out in so many ways including a ride to the airport in Phoenix to the old Terminal Two with its mural of the Phoenix Bird.

The flight from Phoenix arrived in Miami at 1:30 a.m.; the airport was colorful as ever, very international in flavor, old, and full of diverse characters. We would be traveling on Aero Condor, the economy (if I can be euphemistic) airline of Colombia. Avianca was the line wealthy people flew on, and Aero Condor had a reputation for carrying dope and breaking down. It turns out that Avianca did its share of dope carrying over the years as well—hashish, marijuana, cocaine, etc., all big cash exports to the US market by the cartels. This reminds me, the memory is fragile, but I think the old Republic films of Roy Rogers days, those old B cowboy "oaters," used a condor logo. In Colombia when the advertisements for Aero Condor came on the movie screen everyone made a hissing sound and waved their arms, flapping like a bird. We took this airline because it was less expensive and according to good friend Jim Emery had no regulations whatsoever for baggage, although I don't know how that would have affected us. Said rule however may be perhaps a clue why the airline would be investigated and run out of business eventually. Maintenance was supposed to be done in Miami; the airplanes were old 707s and painted a vivid orange.

The aircraft of our departing flight from Miami was filthy inside and smelled as well; it was totally unkempt. We piled in along with other economy passengers (you can tell them by the company they keep); the pilot revved up the engines, taxied out to the runway and then taxied back in. It possibly was an auspicious beginning to our trip. There was a three hour delay in the airport which was freezing cold from a more than efficient air conditioning system (Miami?). We passed some of the time talking with a pleasant Colombian family from Kansas City, the father being the consul there. By departure time we were already absolutely exhausted and miserable, much like one of my visits to Guatemala in 1970 but AFTER a fourteen hour flight from Rio. "The problem was electrical," the unkempt, unprofessional looking mechanic announced at the front of the passenger cabin, dressed in an old green baseball cap like the ones I might use when painting the house. We received a breakfast "vale" and got a bite at a counter where the cook dripped bacon grease on his fingers, waitresses slammed plates around and generally irritated the customers. An omen?

We were back on the flight at 8 a.m. for departure. The liquor cart was "a la Brasileña" with liter bottles of whiskey serving the stuff straight in water glasses. Keah was a bit less nervous after one of those; my scotch was definitely "nacional" and not from Scotland. One can tell by the taste and the ensuing headache. The heating and the air conditioning in the plane seemed to be on at the same time, each coming out of separate vents, but we awoke from a nap nearly frozen. The plane passed over Jamaica with its mountainous terrain which did not seem particularly green at that time of year. Later, flying semi-low over the Colombian main land, all seemed mountainous and craggy as the plane followed the Río Medellín into the Valle del Cauca, our entry point in Colombia. The view was indeed magnificent with Aero Condor flying relatively low and zigzagging through the narrowest canyon I have ever traversed in a jet. I would compare it loosely to a 707 in the Grand Canyon. The jet-jockey was getting the most out of his plane and giving us a few thrills to boot. Keah had wet-palm syndrome with a clammy touch.

ARRIVAL IN MEDELLÍN

Keah and Aero Condor 707

So we landed in Medellín. Customs took one hour and seemed totally inefficient with only one clerk at the entryway to check passports for the passengers of an entire airplane. One had to show proof of a round-trip ticket and money for the stay in the country. This was of course prior to the days of dope running in the late 1970s and 1980s. Customs seemed to be mainly on the lookout for hippy types coming for the local drugs.

The Intercontinental Hotel, Medellín, and Its "Amateur" Bull Ring

We decided to begin the trip, so to speak, at the top, so we went by taxi to a high overlook over Medellín to the Hotel Intercontinental. This was the largest "splurge" on the trip. It was geographically and otherwise "all downhill from there," at least in regard to hotel tariffs. The hotel was a magnificent place with entry hall, lobby, diverse restaurants, colonial style furniture, beautiful pool and green garden area with orchids, tropical plants and even a mini-zoo. And there was a miniature bull fight arena where guests could try their skills with calves instead of ferocious fighting bulls. Most magnificent was the view of the city of Medellín at sunset with its skyscrapers and mountains to the west. The room per se was quite comfortable, much like that in an old fashioned North American hotel, but with the look of luxury on the rest of the premises. Since we had not stayed at a four or five star hotel before and would do so only much later in travels in Brazil, we did not realize that this hotel was typical in that rooms at the best hotels in Latin America at that time, although quite comfortable and nice, generally did not match U.S. standards of "luxury," and that the lobbies, grounds, etc. are the most impressive points of such hotels. A case in point on a trip to Brazil in 1985 would be the Othon Palace in Rio, the hotel facing and rising far above Copacabana beach but with relatively simple rooms. We began the experience with a walk out to the "azotea" or roof garden to see the sunset and then walked through the magnificent gardens below.

There was a light dinner (because of exhaustion) of "churracso" (meat on a spit), fried potatoes and salad. We entertained ourselves much of the evening observing what apparently was the "crème de la crème" of Medellín enjoying a lavish, outdoor dinner and dance in the gardens of the hotel. Many guests arrived with "botas" or wine carriers of leather (as in Spain) or an interesting variant: what looked like a cow's hoof, hollow inside, for the wine. They partied and we went to bed.

Sunday

After a breakfast of juice, ham, eggs, pineapple, hot tea and Danish at the Intercontinental, we took a taxi to mass at a part of Medellín called Poblado with a church with a beautiful wooden altar. One might mention that in 1975 Keah and I were at the height of a very religious time in our lives; church and tradition meant a lot to us. There followed a return to the hotel and drinks by a gorgeous pool with cabanas overlooking the valley. It was a short walk on the hotel grounds to the "macarenita" or little bull ring where amateurs could try their luck at the "corrida" with calves instead of bulls. The name made me think of the "mariconera," the "bolsa" or hand bag men in Spain and Europe carry for cigarettes, documents, etc. Don't ask me why. The "mariconera" is a little joke by Spaniards at their own expense; it means "gay man's purse."

There was a small zoo on the grounds that had macaws, monkeys, llamas, and parrots. As we checked out of the hotel that day (how we would remember that place!), walking into the lobby from the elevator, there appeared three "matadors" in their full "trajes de luces" set for the four o'clock p.m. bull fight in the main ring in Medellín. It was an exciting scene since that aspect of Spanish culture was relatively new to me, except for the novice or "novillero" bull fight I witnessed in the summer of 1962 in Mexico City. Keah was a bit "goggle-eyed" taking it all in for the first time. On a Sunday afternoon drive with Colombian friends we met on the plane (they had migrated to Chicago) we saw the Vera Cruz church dating from the 16th century and the Basílica Metropolitana which was huge but not particularly beautiful. Then we came to the Plaza Bolívar, our first in Colombia; we would soon realize every town had a Bolívar Plaza.

Later on, now from our more modest middle-range hotel, we walked downtown for a "paseo" and ended up eating at "La Magdalena," a Spanish restaurant decorated with posters, photos and memorabilia of famous "toreadores," including El Cordobés and Paco Camino. This was just the first bullfight themed restaurant among many in Colombia. We split a "paella" with yellow rice, squid, a few shrimp, chicken and miscellaneous "mariscos." It turns out Colombia is still a stronghold of certain Spanish traditions, one of them being the bullfight, popular I think in only a few Spanish American countries.

We spent most of the next day at Aero Condor making hotel reservations, flight reservations, etc. for our Colombia trip, the first being a local tour to Santa Fé de Antioquia. For tourism we did a long bus ride which passed through the industrial area of Medellín, seeing brick factories, and gradually climbing to the suburb of Itagüi. The ride reminded me of poor suburbs of Recife in

Brazil, as well as the manner of dress of the people we saw. There were continuous streets of very poor row houses.

Suddenly we arrived at the "ranchito," a beautiful country place in the suburbs, high above the main city, with green, lush pastures where cattle grazed and there was a tremendous view of the mountains surrounding the city. There was a Spanish-style colonial mansion of two floors with wooden balconies, lush gardens and a swimming pool. An ex-president's wife lives there. We then were guided through the gardens with their orchids, the latter few in number but absolutely magnificent (how many times had I gone to the "Jardim Botânico" in Rio de Janeiro and each time was told that "it's out of season." "O senhor deve voltar mais tarde no ano").The orchids ranged from extremely small and delicate to large, all flowering in April and May. The garden was the most beautiful I had seen up to that point in Latin America.

On the return trip we saw the train station, a huge market and experienced a colossal traffic jam. The buses in Medellín were much like their folkloric cousins in Mexico, extremely brightly colored on the outside and decorated with little angels and flowers above the dash. The drivers were without uniforms and seemed poor and unkempt.

Then there was a visit to several folk art shops in the center of town; they sported leather goods, purses, and silver pieces with orchid motifs. A "paseo" on Calle Junín followed; it was a mall affair with many flower stalls for downtown shoppers. Dinner was at "Chun Wah;" it was quiet and we then moved on to a "Robin Hood" joint across the street for ice cream with a surprise inside—bubble gum! It is the small happening that adds the spice to such travels.

"PASEO" TO SANTA FÉ DE ANTIOQUIA, COLOMBIAN PROVINCE OF ANTIOQUIAN INDEPENDENCE

We checked out of the Hotel Bolívar (what other name is possible?) amidst a state of pandemonium. As we were preparing to leave, three busloads of little people arrived; they turned out to be Ecuadoreans, most of Indian ethnicity. All seemed to be in a mad rush with their luggage jamming the only elevator. It was a real panic scene with little people scurrying around like ants; one wondered if their rooms were "first come, first serve." An aside: on our overnight trips in Colombia we had to leave our "big" suitcases in deposits in the hotels; this was a bit unnerving in the Hotel Bolívar since the "depósito" turned out to be the bathroom of the administration.

Keah Smelling the Roses at the Medellín Bus Station

This was our first trip to discover colonial Colombia. We were traveling light (I could not do this today as of this writing)—my briefcase with a toothbrush and change of underwear and a

9

shirt; Keah with all her belongings in her big purse. We walked through a vile part of downtown Medellín (I doubt if I would repeat that trek now) in a "barrio" called Guayaquil. It used to be a market and was without doubt the filthiest part of the city. There were lots of poor people, lots of shady looking characters and Keah and I were trying (ha!) to not look "foreign." The bus station, at best, was a slum. Buses were of the school bus size, gaudy and a bit beat-up in appearance. We managed to get on the right bus which was incidentally jammed to the rafters, people jockeying for position, as there were of course no assigned seats. We sat next to a man sporting a machete in a leather case and carrying a "carriel" containing a Chihuahua dog.

The bus passed through middle class residential areas and then in front of pretty country houses on the sides of the mountains outside of Medellín. The homes looked back to a beautiful view of the city. Soon there were extreme inclines and we indeed felt like we were in the middle of the Andes. There were many flower farms along the slopes. Soon we were up over the top of the sierra and before a sudden expanse of "barrancas," inclines leading into steep canyons. Large flower gardens abounded and there were pine trees but of a fleecy foliage I did not recognize. The road had a good asphalt surface most of the way except for one or two slide areas; we would become extremely familiar with the latter before the end of the trip. There was not much sign of intensive farming but there were cattle, corn, banana trees and later on, tropical fruit trees. There were short stops in Palmita way up on top of the sierra and then San Jerónimo before our final destination of Santa Fé de Antioquia.

This town is of much renown in Colombia and those in the know about Spanish America. It was founded in 1541 by Marshall Jorge Rebledo. It is also known as the site of the original signing of independence of the Province of Antioquia in Colombia from Spain in 1813 and was the capital of Antioquia Province until that title passed to Medellín in the early 19th century. It is in addition the scene of the writer Andés Bello's famous (in certain rather select literary circles) "El Cultivo del Maíz en Antioquia" ("The Growing of Corn in Antioquia"). This poem is found in the principal anthologies of Latin American verse and for some reason is indelibly engraved upon my memory, probably from the survey course of Latin American Literature at Rockhurst University in Kansas City, Missouri. The town seemed to be perfectly preserved in the colonial tradition: cobblestone streets, 16th and 17th century churches, all seemingly little changed from years ago. It was very warm during the day, but a delightful evening breeze allowed for a walk through the central plaza, starkly quiet after the hustle and bustle of Medellín. An aside: more and more, as the trip progressed, we would crave silence and small, out of the way places, a respite from the screeching noise of the large cities.

La Basílica, Santa Fé de Antioquia

We saw the Basílica, "typical" colonial houses and patios, and the church of Santa Bárbara along with its creepy organist. The latter was the old Jesuit Church; the order had been thrown out of Latin America including all Spanish and Portuguese dominions in 1767 as a result of church politics. In this instance during our visit the local Legion of Mary were all in the front pews, singing hymns accompanied by a foot-pumped antique organ. The mass thanks to the girls was beautifully sung, birds were singing outside and it was all very, very tranquil. The tranquility of the town would probably turn to boredom if one were to stay long, but for a short visit it was delightful.

That evening we returned to our colonial style hotel (we were the only guests that day), swam in the pool, had beers and talk by the pool and a late dinner of rice, fries, steak, pineapple-orange salad and wonderful French bread. A large mural of Antioquia decorated the wall of the open air restaurant of the hotel; two gorgeous macaws were ensconced on their perch right outside the window of our room. We returned to the plaza after dinner, enjoying the walk with the cool, calm night breeze. The hotel had a large interior patio with ancient, huge, shade trees and a colonnaded outside patio. It was a good day, medicine for the soul.

I awoke at 4:00 a.m., but it was delightful to hear the country sounds: cocks crowing, birds singing; it all took me back to the days of my youth on the farm near Abilene, Kansas. The a.m. was very cool and pleasant and we were not anxious to leave Antioquia. Another sound in the small town was the pealing of bells of the Basilica, the main timepiece for the entire town. Imagine 400 years marked by the pealing of the same bells and the slow pace and tranquility of it all.

Colonial Residential Architecture, Santa Fé de Antioquia

The illustrations show the town: colonial residences with wooden balconies, tiled roofs, the classic Colombian-Spanish interior patio of brick "ladrillo" floor with a central fountain, flowers all about, and many orchids in planters hung from beams, all good for the soul. The nicer homes have carved doorways, colonial style lamps, wooden "vigas" or decorative beams, wooden lattice work on the windows and entrances to the interior patios. Imagine a modest, small version of the Torre-Tagle Palace in Lima.

So Santa Fe was the place of the original declaration of independence from Spain in this "department" or "province" of old Colombia, and remains as a sample of early colonial residential and religious architecture.

THE RETURN TRIP TO MEDELLÍN

For a change we had a good bus driver, unhurried, chatting with passengers, a rare "bird" amongst his colleagues. Some pretty Colombian girls got on at San Jerónimo; they turned out to be "normalistas" or grade-school teachers who rode the bus from Medellín to country roads leading to small villages where they teach in rural schools. One recalls the mystique of the heroine-rural school teacher in Mexico after the Revolution of 1910—their mission to alphabetize the poor—and the old Mexican movie with Dolores del Río playing the part. The countryside on the return was beautiful; Medellín is in the famous "Valle del Cauca" of Colombia. There were "Zebu" or Brahma cattle, papayas, bananas, etc. San Jerónimo along the way was a small country town with one long row of houses on the main street and with a pretty flowered plaza. The people seemed modestly dressed but clean, though perhaps poor. It offered a very different impression from, let's say, Northeastern Brazil where the poverty is so much more visible. Is this naïve? Or perhaps impressionistic? It was a bit of a shock when the bus stopped suddenly in the middle of a jungle-like area in front of a path and a small clearing and a pretty, young, Colombian woman dressed to kill in the latest of urban clothing got on the bus!

We are traveling along and over one range of the Andes at this point. How different from the Peru I remember from 1967! Here it is totally and beautifully green with thick grass pasturing livestock, many, many plantations, and banana trees to the horizon; all at around an altitude of 8000 feet we are told. Once again we saw the flower gardens on the slopes outside Medellín. What cannot be reproduced on slides or paper is the enormous grandeur of the Andes.

We experienced no troubles at the infamous bus station in Medellín, but arrived exhausted to the Hotel Bolívar. The Ecuadorean horde seemed nowhere in sight, so all was calm. Breakfast at the restaurant was "cacerola de huevos fritos," fried eggs cooked in a small fry pan and served in the same at table. We had lunch at the fast food joint, Robin Hood, a Colombian hamburger, and then took a bus to the Botanical Gardens of Medellín. Once again there was an amazing collection of orchids, better or at least rivaling that of "El Ranchito" a few days (it seemed like months) past.

Jesus Nazareno Church, Medellín

We returned to the downtown and got off the bus too early, but it turned out well because we were able to walk to the Jesus Nazareno Church and get ashes ("cenizas") on Ash Wednesday. It seemed an ostentatious show of piety, I thought, with the entire forehead smeared with the black stuff, not nearly as dainty as in U.S. Catholicism. As time went by and we saw much more of Colombia, I believe that the Catholic view of the dark side of suffering, penitence and the like held sway and still holds sway in much of Colombia. In 1975 the country was stereotyped as the most conservative and traditional of the Latin American Catholic countries. I wrote in 1975, "Thus far we have seen little of the Post-Vatican II Church here. The rebel priest Camilo Torres was killed in 1966 and remains as a symbol of the radical guerrilla church in Latin America."

Keah enjoyed a white coconut treat, and we returned to the Paseo in downtown Medellín for two hours near Calle Junín: there were old gentlemen types in dark suits and tie whiling away the hours, couples, some bums, shoe-shine boys, and girls in the style of the day (do you recall the platform shoes worn by women and men of the 1970s?). And the photos show the "bell bottom" trousers of both men and women in the style of the times. The plaza on Calle Junín reminded me a bit of the markets and plazas of Northeast Brazil with the poets and the fire eaters. Much curiosity was directed toward us since I think most tourists do not simply stop, sit and observe. We were in no hurry. There were young girls in tight fitting clothes and platform shoes letting themselves be seen, as is the custom in those parts. We walked to the infamous Edificio Coletec Medellín and took the elevator to the 34th floor to see sights in the city. (This is the building that had the disastrous fire some years back, burning from the middle of the building with people trapped above). A similar thing happened in Bogotá at the time. We returned to "ChanWah" for "arroz con camarones" while staring at its aquariums.

February 13. It was time for the departure from Medellín after this pleasant visit prior to the days of the drug cartel; the jet was from Aero Condor and commenced an incredibly short flight up the mountain to Bogotá. There was an unusual impression from this flight: the plane took off, went into a very steep climb, leveled off over a green savannah, and ripped on into the Bogotá airport.

BOGOTÁ

We were met at the airport by our host Jim Emery's father who took us in his Nissan Jeep to the family's comfortable apartment where we met all the family. Later there was a quick introductory ride about the city: up the "cerro" or mountain surrounding the city to view the city and the other side, the route to the "llanos" or plains to the east and south. And we also saw the shrine to the "Vírgen de la Candelaria" up on top.

An aside: here is a vignette from the Bogotá airport and the Third World's fascination with gadgets, circa 1975. A wealthy Colombian tourist, recently returned from where I do not know, was fiddling with an amazing camera set-up: he had a tripod and much equipment and was studiously set up in one of the many lobbies of the airport, focusing on the wall. It was a plain, tiled wall with no frescos or the like, just a wall. Perhaps he was preparing himself for greater things, but the fascination with mechanical things, gadgets and the like, I believe, simply overcame him while waiting for one of those interminably late flights in Bogotá airport.

An important first stop the next day was a visit to the "Almacén Roka" where we made our first purchase of Colombian "ruanas"—the blanket-like poncho with a slit in the middle for the head, made of very high quality wool in subtle or brilliant colors. These are worn by both men and women in the very cool and at times downright cold climate of Bogotá. Recall Bogotá is at about 8000 feet altitude. I was surprised to see businessmen in conservative dark suits and ties with a black or dark "ruana" as a sort of topcoat. Ours were used throughout the trip as extra blankets for warmth on long bus rides over the Andes and in hotel rooms as extra bedding. Upon our return they turned out to be perfect for the slightly cool winters in Phoenix. Keah, the good shopper, was overcome with the vast selection and spent an inordinate amount of time on her own selection.

We returned "home" to the Emery's house on the local "buseta" (mini-bus) "que se baró" or broke down in the traffic. The quandaries of being a linguist traveling in Latin America reared their ugly head: "buseta" in Colombian Spanish and "buceta" (the same pronunciation) in Brazilian Portuguese have slightly different meanings. The first, in Colombia, means "a small, school-type bus." The second, in Brazil, in vulgar and slang terms means "female sex organ." So imagine the Brazilian tourist for the first time in Bogotá who is told in Spanish (the two languages are so close, right? and all Brazilians understand Spanish, right?): Take the "buseta" on the corner" or the Colombian in Brazil who innocently asks a bystander: "Where do I find the nearest "buseta?" While I'm at it: the trilled double R in Spanish is aspirated in Brazilian Portuguese, thus in Brazil the word "to run," "correr," is pronounced like the Spanish "coger." But "coger" in Mexico is a colorful, vulgar expression for the standard run of the mill sex act, i.e. the "f" word. One runs into situations where you hear a Brazilian say, "Yes we are "into" exercise: "Todos correm nas praias.'" "Indeed," says the Mexican tourist.

Anyway, the Colombian "buseta" broke down and we returned home in a wild taxi ride, one among many on the trip.

Bogotá, founded in the 1500s by conqueror Gonzalo Jiménez de Quesada, in 1975 had approximately three million inhabitants. It is in a long valley or "sabana" on a plateau of the Andes, the valley about thirty miles long. Downtown is centered at the foot of a steep mountain called Monserrate (from the same name as the Virgin in Spain "La Virgen de Monserrate"). Streets running parallel to the mountains are called "carreras;" streets running perpendicular are called "calles." But . . . the name "avenida" can be used for certain "calles" and "carreras." Therefore, "Calle 40A-28-40" intersects with KRA 28, forty meters from the corner. Got it? There was considerable pollution in the city, but not anything like good 'ole Phoenix. The view up to the mountains was beautiful.

Colonial Spanish architecture predominates, but we saw sections of town near our hosts' house with English, Swiss and other European motifs. Downtown itself is huge and is agitated with crowds. So the city center of Bogotá is a mixture of sky scrapers and colonial style buildings. Much of the older part of the city has been leveled and modern buildings take its place. But the city fathers have had the good sense to preserve much of the colonial heritage, as we shall soon see.

Traffic like in any other large city is a mess. There was an incredible variety of buses, taxis, and cars of all vintages. Basic urban transportation is a problem due to the influx of population from the country. Public transportation was very cheap compared to the U.S., particularly the buses which run crowded most of the time. A few times we were packed in like pickled herrings. And Bogotá in the 1970s had some fame as the center for the "gamines" or street urchins. There are literally tens of thousands of homeless children who sleep in the streets and make their living as petty thieves. They work in pairs and are a menace to the unwary shopper and particularly the tourist. Our hosts the Emerys tell of people stopping at a stop light in their car. One of the thieves pounds on the trunk of the car, the driver turns around, and in a flash the second thief reaches in the door and snatches the purse or whatever. No one wears exposed jewelry on the streets, another convenient reason for the "ruana" over clothing I suppose. There are horror stories of slashed wrists when thieves on scooters or motor bikes cut the watches off the arms of drivers who happen to have the window open as they zoom past. So this is the atmosphere that awaited us. But with caution, all turned out well.

Burglaries in private residences were rampant, and no one in their right mind leaves a vehicle parked on the street at night, that is, without a plethora of locks. In spite of a series of five heavy padlocks on the new Nissan (on the ignition, the steering column, gear shift, etc.) the Emerys' jeep was stolen shortly after we left. The main door to their apartment had four or five heavy padlocks and diverse other locks.

Streets, bus stations, and even the airport are infamous for thieves. We were on buses with other North American tourists whose passports were stolen while they traveled (at night I suspect). We had no problems but took precautions.

OUR HOSTS THE EMERYS

The Emery Family, Bogotá

Mr. Emery is a graduate in architecture from Princeton. It was later that he received his calling as a missionary for the Presbyterian Church. His wife Elaine is of equal faith. The family has been in Colombia for many years, and his main task is to build churches throughout the country as well as evangelize. Her main task is to establish Christian Fellowship with women's groups, Bible Study and the like. In spite of their not uncertain opposition to the Colombian Catholic hierarchy, we got along famously with them. One son, John, is a graduate of Harvard Business School. My former student Jim is a graduate of Arizona State University with a degree in Economics. One daughter is married to a Colombian who is an accountant.

Mr. Emery, Lorentz or "Lorenzo," has been 28 years in Colombia and remembers well the "violencia" of the late 1940s when a state of civil war existed for years between liberals and conservatives with widespread bloodshed and thousands of lives lost. The war basically lasted from 1948 to 1953 and was followed by the 16 year agreement ("El Convenio de los 16 Años") when both factions agreed to alternate power. A by-product in the 1960s was the rebel groups, many Marxist oriented; it was the epoch of Camilo Torres, a famous Marxist priest in Colombia. The President in 1975 was López Michelson, "el liberal que se vuelve cada vez más conservador," "the liberal who seems each time more conservative."

Permit an aside: this story does not follow Colombian political life for the many years since this trip in 1975, but suffice to say "things turned south." The Guerrilla rebel group FARC became stronger with political violence, kidnappings and such, and then came the Colombian Cartel. I have it that things are much better today in 2012.

LOOKING FOR THE COLONIAL HERITAGE IN BOGOTÁ

La Casa del Marqués de San Jorge, Bogotá

LA CASA DEL MARQUÉS DE SAN JORGE

We took the bus downtown to, what else? Plaza Bolívar through an unsafe part of town according to Jim; the emerald black market dealers frequent this area and occasional shootings are not uncommon! So we were in the old city dating back to the 16th century.

The first site was the famous Casa del Marqués de San Jorge which the Colombians humbly acclaim to be the best example of colonial architecture in Bogotá. Although built in the late 16th and 17th centuries, it had been rebuilt in the 18th and 19th century styles and that latter construction has been maintained. Today it is a museum of popular ceramics. It sported the usual tiled roof and a labyrinth of rooms on two levels connected by wooden staircases. There were the usual wooden balconies, several internal patios with brick floors throughout, Moorish arches and fountains. We saw ceramics from Peru, Ecuador and Mexico and a large display of colonial furniture.

El Capitolio, Bogotá

EL PALACIO NACIONAL DE GOBIERNO

After the capitol building we walked nearby to the national palace with the guards in front, all in blue uniforms and all with sub-machine guns and wearing helmets in the Prussian Army style of the mid-nineteenth century. It turns out that diverse Latin American countries modeled their national armies after the German or Prussian models, including dress. There were black Mercedes automobiles all around the palace itself. The entrance foyer sported a large, ornate candelabra and red carpeting throughout. Our vision was blocked to the interior. This is the same place which was attacked by rebels in 1985 and several dignitaries were killed in the battle.

Baroque Entryway, Museo Colonial, Bogotá

EL MUSEO COLONIAL

This is the most famous museum in Bogotá and is located in the area already described. As often the case in Latin America since the demise (temporary) of the Jesuit Order expelled in 1767, the building is an old convent once owned by the Jesuits, connecting to the Iglesia de San Ignacio. Its patios were full of flowers, and there was a beautiful fountain. The outer walls were surrounded by the walls of several other churches. There were diverse salons with paintings by Vásquez y Ceballos, the most famous painter of the colonial period, jewels of the period, and furniture of the Viceroys.

Portrait of One of the Famous Viceroys of Nueva Granada, Colonial Museum, Bogotá

Santa Fé de Bogotá was one of the four vice-royalties established by Spain in the New World. The others were Nueva España in Mexico, Peru in Lima, both in the 16th century, and Río de la Plata in Buenos Aires in the 18th, the same century as Nueva Granada with the main city of Bogotá. There was a large salon with the portraits of all the viceroys. Significant was a special gallery of wooden, carved statues of the 16th to the 18th centuries, primarily religious art: figures of the Virgin and the saints, all in Andalusian, or the Cuzco or Quiteño styles prominent in the period. One sees a concert hall with various pianos, its walls covered with paintings by Vásquez-Arce y Ceballos. At the entrance was a large, carved gold-gilt altar from the colonial period. In addition, there was a salon with colonial furniture from some duchess; of note was the tiny, diminutive bed—short people in those days! I recall the gold-gilt, carved entryway to the museum, taken I imagine, from one of the old churches. Thievery from the churches is another story for later.

I believe one has to be particularly interested in this sort of thing, i.e. artifacts from the Spanish colonial period. Frankly, the images of the many viceroys and royal personages and the endless religious paintings wore on me after a while, and the many slides taken were not a favorite of students in the later civilization classes at Arizona State University. Per chance the Gold Museum would be of more interest. It would have to wait after lunch.

We enjoyed a lunch of "churrasco," beef cooked over "brasas' or coals, barbecued chicken, rice, potatoes, salad, bread and washed down with Colombian beer. The cost was $2.00 U.S. for both of us. The music was piped in to the restaurant and seemed familiar to my ear—tapes of Brazilian star singer Roberto Carlos singing in Spanish.

THE GOLD MUSEUM

We spent the p.m. in Bogotá's famous Gold Museum ("Museo de Oro)." The collection is comprised of 15,000 pieces, without doubt the largest in the world of its kind. The items are from the principal pre-Colombian tribes of Colombia and Panama. Keep in mind Panama only came into existence at the point of the U.S. construction of the Panama Canal a little after 1900. And not without controversy; the land area of Panama previously was part of Colombia. It is believed that Colombian gold (not the herbal but the real stuff) arrived at the Plaza of Tenochtitlán in the Mexico City of the Aztecs in those days and that trade of such objects took place through all of Central America. The museum, by the way, also possessed five of the largest emeralds found in the world at a value in 1975 of 18 million dollars. Emeralds were worth more than diamonds, and Colombia is the largest producer.

One could see that gold was used primarily as an adornment, but also for cult objects and as a container for "coca" and lime used in the times. There were ornaments for the nose, ears, breast, neck and even helmets of gold. There is one room, a vault actually, full of gold and emeralds which must rival the famous Incan temple of the Coricancha, that legendary temple filled with gold at the request of the Conquistador Pizarro in Peru as ransom for the Inca Prince Atahualpa who was captured by the Spaniards and used to bring the Inca Empire to its feet. The Incas supposedly filled the temple with gold, but this only whetted the Spaniards' appetite for more. Poor Atahualpa was executed anyway, a sad story.

The Golden Raft, "La Balsa de Oro," Museo de Oro, Bogotá

The most impressive piece in the museum for me was the "Raft of Gold" ("La Balsa de Oro") interpreted by experts as the depiction of the original legend of "The Gold One" ("El Dorado"). There appears to be an Indigenous chieftain standing on the raft, accompanied by lesser nobility or priests (all this is a matter of conjecture). The "balsa" logs of the raft are actually all made of gold. In fact the entire thing is entirely of gold and was only recently discovered by a farmer in a cave or "guaca" in the Colombian countryside. El Dorado refers of course to the legend of the priest dressed in gold, or perhaps with body painted in gold, seated on a raft filled with gold and emeralds. The chief is taken to a deep lake where he and the gold are sacrificed to the gods. Another version of the legend is that he bathes in the water, washing off the gold, and tosses all the gold and emeralds into the water as an offering. Mryiad stories have been written of the phenomenon and they are just that—stories. At any rate the legend spread like wildfire in 16th century Europe and literally dozens of treasure hunters—Spanish, English, French, and Dutch—died hunting the elusive treasure. Such goings on took place all over the South American continent, including the deepest forested parts of the Amazon. There is a lake, Guataita by name if memory serves, close to Bogotá and some believe this could be the one of the legend! It is a nice story with huge consequences. One version has it that the golden raft was unearthed by a Colombian farmer plowing his field with oxen; he heard a "thunk" and there you have it.

I have seen many interesting museums, but none like this one. It is in the Banco de Bogotá building, not entirely an accident of nature.

Church of San Francisco, Bogotá

THE CHURCH OF THE THIRD ORDER OF ST. FRANCIS

Across the street from the Gold Museum is one of the most impressive churches we saw in Colombia: the Third Order of St. Francis, coincidentally the same order as that in Salvador da Bahia in Brazil with its outstanding baroque church. The interior was built entirely of "nogal," walnut I think, and "cedro," cedar. There was a reddish hue throughout, and the style was "Morisco." Impressive also was the Colombian good taste: there was piped in Bach as we sat and admired the scene. Such churches throughout Colombia seemed more museums than places of worship, not uncommon in Latin America.

THE CHURCH OF SAN FRANCISCO

The Church of San Francisco is to its side. We attended mass at San Francisco Church. The Viceroys were inaugurated here! And Bolívar took power here as well. The original church was under construction from 1550 to 1565. Images of saints are from Barcelona and carved confessionals are from Castille. The main altar was done in 1662 by an Austurian, carved from wood and covered with gold paint. Also of note in the church was the seat or throne of the Viceroy and the altar of Our Lady "La Imaculada" called "Nuestra Señora de Guasa" by the Indians with the sun as her crown and the moon resting at her feet. This image was never damaged or attacked in any of the Indian conflicts during the conquest. The diverse altars were all in gold gilt, baroque style. The Christ figure of Monserrate was formerly here before being taken up the mountain to its present shrine overlooking Bogotá. In effect, the Church of the Third Order spoken of previously was an addition to this church and done in 1761. As mentioned, it was done all in walnut and cedar by the architect Pedro Caballero who retired upon its completion and then went crazy! Such anecdotes are replete throughout Colombia—more to come!

LA IGLESIA DE LA VERA CRUZ

The pilgrimage goes on. We then went to the Iglesia de la Vera Cruz, the oldest church still standing in the city, actually built by the conquistadors, dating from 1546. It was in Romanesque style (simpler) done by the "Hermandad de la Santa Agonía" who had as their mission the consoling of those condemned to death; one surmises by the Inquisition. It is unclear if the death penalty was for crimes or the Inquisition or what. They must have been busy. The church was white inside, simple, with rounded altars. The ceiling was of Moorish style. Seventy martyrs have been buried under the nave since Independence from Spain.

THE CATHEDRAL OF BOGOTÁ

The list goes on and on. I think we wanted to get it all over with in one day. We went to the Cathedral of Bogotá on whose site was originally constructed the first church in the city, straw roof and all. The church was built by Don Gonzalo Jiménez de Quesada, founder of the city and conqueror of Colombia, and his remains lie in place below the altar. The church is simple in style with high columns, a choir loft of carved wood, but all in all it was dirty, cold and cavernous. A mass was celebrated (it was Sunday in downtown Bogotá) with perhaps fifteen people in attendance with a priest that I surmise not even natives could understand, taking into consideration the lousy p.a. system. There was a huge iron or brass knocker (shades of "Young Frankenstein" by Mel Brooks) on the principal door, in the form of a lion. The place seemed more like a tomb than a church. For any Spanish majors, it elicits a comment: this would have given Luis de Góngora,"The Prince of Darkness" of the Spanish Baroque poetry of the 17th century, a wonderful opportunity for one of his linked metaphors: . . . if not a tomb . . . then a church . . . !

CHURCH OF THE JESUITS

Do not desist oh faint of heart! Would you believe one more church this day? We went to the Jesuit Church (save the best for last!) It was elegant with beautiful paintings throughout. But the outstanding point, according to Colombian guides, is the painting of Velásquez y Páramo. It was, in my humble and uneducated opinion, the best collection of sacred art in Bogotá, including its murals in the chapel of St. Joseph. Leave it to the Jesuits, or perhaps, what is left of the Jesuits. One needs to know the story of their forced departure from all Portuguese and Spanish possessions in 1767 decreed by the Marquez de Pombal in Lisbon. The excellent movie "The Mission" with Robert de Niro and Jeremy Irons depicts one aspect of the Jesuit story.

All this religion made us hungry for material things, so there was a lunch of chicken and rice and a return to the home base "due to the cold." We had a siesta and then a walk to the National Park which was beautiful, green and full of people for a Sunday p.m. stroll. Behind it loomed the beautiful view of the mountains including that of Monserrate.

THE "MUSEO NACIONAL"

Another day, another monument. It was gigantic and impossible to absorb in one day. There were four sections: ethnography, archeology, history and fine arts. It was founded by good ole' General Santander in 1823; before that it was a prison.

The first floor housed typical clothing from various departments of Colombia, crafts and arts from different indigenous cultures, including the Arawak, Tolima and Chibcha.

Second floor: History. Salón de las Banderas, Bolívar room, Gran Colombia room, conquest room, colony room. There were arms and the armor of Jiménez de Quesada, conquistador "número uno" of Colombia, heavy, beautiful and with mail. And there was the mantle of the wife of Atahualpa the "last" Inca chieftain. And also one saw the crown of gold that was offered to Bolívar in Cuzco, this for his efforts as one of the great leaders of Independence in Latin America, and Bolívar's last will and testament. Also appearing was a collection of money and coins from the entire history of the country, a huge leather book with "rentas y gastos" (income and expenses) of the Gran Colombia, a short-lived, utopic union of South American states shortly after Independence from Spain. Then there was the Independence Room: paintings, uniforms, arms and furniture from the heroes or leaders of the cause: Nariño, Camilo Torres and what seemed a thousand other generals. General Santander's billiard table too. And finally, the Presidents' room: portraits of them all. Are we exhausted yet?

Third floor. There were paintings from the best artists of Colombia from the colony to the present. Vásquez y Arce, Zubarán, and others. A tourist note: later that day the entire city of Bogotá had an electrical blackout for three hours.

TOURISM IN BOGOTÁ

Downtown Bogotá Skyscrapers

Another outing was to the Universidad de los Andes for my meeting with Dean Charlotte Samper to discuss a possible ASU Summer School program. The campus is on the edge of downtown on a knoll with long, tree-lined walkways. It was modern and beautiful. The conversation went well, but with no commitments on either side.

Then we went to the Instituto Caro y Cuervo, famous in all Latin America for linguistic studies, inspired by the scholar Andrés Bello. Señor Caro y Cuervo did the first grammar of Latin American Spanish. We visited the downtown office; the Institute is actually on a hacienda in the suburbs of Bogotá called Hacienca Yerba Buena, 24 kilometers outside the city. By the way, the Colombians pride themselves on having "the best Spanish" of all Latin America, an idea hotly contested if you are not a Colombian. However, it was indeed a pleasure to speak with the educated Colombians, and I'll second their motion.

The Author in the Plaza de Toros, Bogotá

Then we proceeded to the Plaza Santa María de Toros. It was a memorable experience in that it was empty, but open, so we could enter, sit in the stands and imagine a famous bull fight. I walked down to the arena and Keah took a wonderful picture of me in a "ruana" in the center of the ring looking up to tall apartment buildings surrounding the same with low clouds and mountains in the back. This I am sure is the only time yours truly will be in the middle of a bullfight arena! The museum next door was excellent: there was a "traje de luces" from Paco Cáceres, images of El Cordobés and posters from years ago depicting famous "toreros" from Juan Belmonte to Manolete to Luiz Dominguín to El Cordobés. These are indeed the "heavy hitters" of bull fight history. The bulls were present as well, their heads that is, and one or two without their ears, awarded posthumously to the brave toreros who did them in.

The next day we did a short "paseo" to the north zone of Bogotá: the soccer stadium, the basketball stadium and various upper class residential areas, the latter placed at the foot of the hills and mountains, all very elegant. On the top of the hill, now barren of trees but quite green, one looked over into the state of Boyacá, an important area we would visit later. There one saw lots of trees, and haciendas in the green distance, all very beautiful.

The matter of real estate in Bogotá: we went through a Spanish-Colonial style house which was for sale: three living rooms, three fireplaces, innumerable sleeping rooms on perhaps six split levels. Estimated value: $50,000 U.S. So Colombia was a good deal in 1975.

In the plaza near the Emerys' house there was a rapid change today; in the space of a few hours all was converted into a scenario for a TV commercial: "Promociones Públicas." Renault planted trees overnight and promised a big, "superior" promotion! Cars arrived from nowhere. Yellow banners proclaimed "Superior!" Twenty trees had been planted and a city truck arrived to water them. That night a band of musicians arrived from the coast with carnival music, much like Brazilian northeastern "caipira" music. Capitalism Colombian style!

We visited the Hotel Tequendama, top of the line in Bogotá at the time with luxury shops including H. Stern and Colombian Emeralds. Then we walked to the nearby Hilton where we witnessed a vignette of upper class Bogotano life: a tea for the ladies with jazz music and accompanying style show, card games, and dice. The "manequins" or models were strictly Latino: elegant and sexy, not thin as U.S. counterparts and not afraid to move around a bit to show off what they've got! Platform shoes were in style, full skirts and heavy makeup.

We then did a long walk home past the Brazilian Embassy with mist, clouds, very cool weather and the tops of the mountains blocked out by the same. Later in the north zone we saw the Bogotá Country Club with its polo fields, flowers everywhere, modern architecture and a mix of European style: Bavarian, Scandinavian, English and a new "shopping center." This is the residential area of North Americans and other diplomats.

We add a vignette on traffic in Bogotá shortly before our first departure from the city. At one of the major intersections in the downtown there are little traffic kiosks from which guards with whistles direct traffic, efficiently waving arms, whistling, etc. to move things along. We caught one scene when no one, absolutely no one at all, would obey the signals of the policeman. He got flustered, moved the wrong row of traffic at the wrong time and horns began to blow. It was a scene right out of Hollywood. A Latino flavor to it all.

After the serious visits to museums and churches, and the more relaxing tourism, it was time to begin the next phase of the "Odyssey."

PART II. TRAVELS TO THE WEST AND SOUTH—PARAPHRASING CERVANTES' "DON QUIXOTE:" "LA PRIMERA SALIDA"

Actually it was the second if you count Santa Fé de Antioquia out of Medellín. Our destination was eventually to be the Pre-Colombian site of San Agustín, but via Girardot, Cali and the famous Popayán.

We guarded our bags zealously at the bus station, ever aware of Bogotá's reputation for thieves; it seemed as gringos we were being watched constantly. The bus departed and not unexpectedly not on schedule making its way through the south part of the city. This was our first time passing through the workers' residential area and the "barrios" or slums. And it was also the industrial part of the city. Then the bus passed through a green savanna area, gradually descending from Bogotá through coffee plantations on both sides of the road. There were banana trees, the orange "wedding flower" trees and many, many country inns called "Paradores." We passed through Milgar with many tourist hotels with pools, quite popular for "Bogotanos" wanting to leave the high, cold city and go to the inns on weekends to swim and take the sun. The bus driver was terrifying. It would be on one of these roads that such a bus would crash head on into the Nissan of Lorenzo Emery who was killed, this just a few months after our trip. He had traveled the roads of Colombia for 28 years before fate caught up with him.

GIRARDOT

The "Liberal" House near Água de Dios

The bus has descended two or three thousand feet from the high, cool savannah of Bogotá to tropical country. We stayed at the house of Linda Buller, an R.N. from the Mennonite area near Hutchinson, Kansas, and currently working at the leper colony in Água de Dios. It was hot and humid and difficult to cool off. The shower water at Linda's house was unheated but felt great. It was back to the tropics after the super cool Bogotá.

The Market, Girardot

The market in Girardot was exceptional. There were two levels, the first with all kinds of tropical fruit and foods, the second a parrot and bird market. There were also tourist curios, the latter junky I thought except for nice woven baskets which caught our attention and were duly noted for possible purchase later. As most such markets in the tropics, it was very dirty, very smelly, but exotic. In other words, it was a good market. Keah noted a roast pig resting on a shelf, and we both wondered how long it had been there.

I was very much affected by the tropical heat and humidity, and a cold shower again at Linda's was welcome upon our return from the market. Her little Spartan apartment is designed for the climate: it was open to fresh air at all points possible and with ventilator fans for cooling. An aside: air conditioning in most places in the tropics, at least on a small residential scale, has not been a happy experience for us. Most air conditioning units are old and the humidity ruins them quickly. They roar in the heat. The simple ceiling fans of days of yore are far more efficient. They are quiet and cooling and meant for the tropics. I recall a cabana hotel on Isla Mujeres, Mexico, with such cooling, a place located near the coral reef. Perfect!

Linda Buller was an exuberant, hard-working, kind, Christian woman. When she first came to Colombia, she worked as a mid-wife in a country town and told that more often than not she was threatened by expectant fathers: "It had better be twins this time or you're gone!" A local custom was to shoot off guns "To Our Lady" during the period of labor in an appeal for a male baby. Since then Linda has been at Água de Dios for ten years where she helped build a school and now makes shoes for the lepers.

CROSSING THE ANDES: THE INFAMOUS ANDEAN "DERRUMBES" OR LANDSLIDES.

We were up early and were off to a very picturesque bus station with a surly station master (he never did let us know when our bus was to leave), shoe shine boys, paper boy, an old fellow "in charge" of luggage, and a taxi stand with a fellow in a genuine old-time taxi hat. There were stewardesses for the luxury buses, much noise amidst the street scenes, all very entertaining if you just sat back and watched.

The bus for Cali was jammed and we drew the very last row of seats. The trip started out in flat country with plowed fields of cotton, all very pretty. Houses were of mud painted white over sticks with thatch roof; many were painted red or blue designating the liberal or conservative political bent during the "Violencia" of the 1940s and 1950s.

We began a gradual climb, arriving in Ibagué. There was no bathroom in the bus station for women, so Keah was indeed in a "tight spot." We always said such things were "to build character." Easy for a man to say.

Then there was a truly amazing ride up into the Andes and over the top of one of the "cordilleras." Note that there are three different "cordilleras" or chains of the Andes in Colombia. All was completely green with high passes, a curved mountain road, and agriculture in terraces at what seemed a 45 degree incline with corn and other crops growing on the sides of the mountains. At the top of one of the passes there was a "bus stop" with a tiny inn-store-bakery. The bathroom was a story in itself: it was a two-holer, but below the holes were open space and a cliff down several hundred feet. You did not want to drop anything like keys, your billfold, or God forbid, your passport, but Keah was happy to discover even these accommodations.

Our driver was amazing, nice enough to chat with, but a maniac behind the wheel. He drove incredibly fast through the mountains, passed continuously, played "pop" Colombian music as loud as he could on the bus's p.a. system (all the buses were wired in Colombia), but in the end seemed to be an alert, Emerson Fittipaldi type of driver.

Landslide in the Andes, Stalled Trucks, Keah, on the Way to Cali

On the way down from the pass our bus stalled for one and one-half hours because of a mud slide, the first we encountered, but the first of many to come. A big truck had jackknifed at the slide, thus closing both lanes. Impatient drivers would pull out of line and attempt to sidle past on the inside or outside and ended up getting mired in the mess. Clouds came in and with them cold air, but fortunately we had the "ruanas" purchased for such an occasion at the Roka Store in Bogotá. There was a long wait for things to be resolved, so we spent part of the time waiting outside the bus for the slide to be cleared. Men were alongside the road taking naps; all the passengers were outside observing the scene since it was impossible to rest in the bus since the music continued to blare in spite of it all. This was the moment when I was serenely passing the time of day, standing outside our bus, gazing across the deep ravine when I heard this pissing sound very near my shoes. I detected a slightly familiar odor and discovered a Colombian to be just as serenely taking a pee very near me. I still wonder if that was his personal protest against Yankee Imperialism or if he simply had to go. Probably the latter. It turns out there is a dearth of facilities throughout the countryside, not to speak of the scenes of unexpected landslides. Men are liable to just "let it go" just about anywhere. (This reminds of the Brazilian saying "Go behind the Statue" "Vá atrás da estátua" in Brazil's Northeast. I always did notice the familiar smell at the public landmarks in the plazas.) But pity the women.

The worst was yet to come. The slide was eventually cleared, the truck dragged to the side, and as George Jones would sing, "The Race was On." All the long line of trucks, buses and other vehicles decided to make up for lost time and race down the mountain. It was terrifying. It seemed akin to the Indianapolis 500: we crept out slowly, all jockeying for position, and then, VARUUM, a terrific pace was set around curves not meant for such a race, all the way down the mountain. And it seemed that 98 per cent of the traffic was trucks or buses.

A bit outside of Cali a tire blew out, and we noted the bus drivers check the tires by banging a rock against them. Seems to work most of the time.

THE CAUCA VALLEY AND CALI

So thus we traversed the long "cordillera" down to lower mountains at Armenia and Calacá. This was now a huge banana and coffee producing area, verdant and lush, which seemed to go on and on. Then we passed through foothills and suddenly the Cauca Valley lay before us. It is a tremendously fertile area; the locals say among the most fertile in the world. There were sugar cane plantations, cattle ranches, fruit production of all kinds and coca and marijuana as well. The valley is very wide and Cali sits at its southwest end.

The big meal or "almuerzo" was at a country inn or "Parador." There was "sancocho," a green concoction strange to my delicate tummy, of rice, papas, yucca (soon a favorite of Keah's) and carne. Note that this dish is both a staple and a delicacy for the Colombians. After the meal, we were both amazed and in a state of shock viewing the bathroom.

We took a taxi from the bus station to our hotel and both noted the extremely loose steering wheel which the driver spun endlessly to steer us in possibly the right direction. There was a minor altercation at our hotel in Cali when we were charged far more than the tourist agent in Bogotá had promised. We had the distinct impression of "getting screwed" once again as tourists. It was a bit of a bummer.

Sunday in Cali

"Mudéjar" Tower on Church, Cali

On Sunday we attended mass at the San Francisco church with its Arabesque towers. The style is called "Mudéjar" thus explaining the arabesque stonework; inside the church there were no statues save on the main altar. The priest spoke in what seemed Baroque syntax. A monk with a speech defect was leading the singing. The speaker system distorted it all so we got very little out of mass. I noted that people would ask for change from the collection basket or simply perform the operation themselves as it passed. A kitty cat crawled up on the central altar and pruned itself during the mass. So it was entertaining in a way. The people in attendance were poor; there was no sign of middle or upper class attendance. One wonders: is this because the church is in the old downtown?

Breakfast was at a tiny café nearby with customers including a deaf-mute, a ragged beggar lady and a whorish type clinging to a boyfriend. She was very "stacked" with short skirt, leather boots with elevator heels, and all in bright red. Such company we keep.

Cali's Plaza Caicedo was very quiet and pretty on a Sunday morning, surrounded by the "Justicia" or courts building; the latter was French in the Neo-Classic style as were other government buildings and the Cathedral. The park was impressive with tall palms, benches, and statues surrounded by skyscrapers.

Mark J. Curran

An unexpected research note. There was a small market where I purchased several popular broadside-style pamphlets, akin to the "cordel" of Brazil. The verse in them is more like that of the "trovadores" or troubadours of southern Brazil and not folkloric as in Brazil's northeast.

Once again there was a minor incident with the hotel personnel and we were glad to be out of there. In a sense it made the Cali stay unfortunate and a bit negative.

ON TO POPAYÁN

We arrived at the bus station for the trip to Popayán, to the south on the road to Ecuador. This time it was the Palmira Line. The back of the bus was full of school girls in uniform. They talked of the yet popular Brazilian singer Roberto Carlos whom they adored: "Es muy romántico!" And they spoke like good junior Rotarians of the beauty of Cali. All knew of the Colombian romantic novel "María" but none had read it. They all flirted, smoked and were cute Latino teens.

The bus continued to pass through the long valley of the Cauca. It was flat, very wet, flooded in many areas with the rivers up and muddy. There were huge expanses of green pasture with Brahma herds and also the black "toros" famously raised in these parts for the "corridas." Cauca's wealth was apparent: the haciendas were neat and very successful looking in appearance. Someone told us that the topsoil reaches depths of 100 feet in this valley! By comparison, I think it is perhaps three to six feet in the Kansas river bottoms.

At the end of the valley we began a gradual climb and the character of the land changed considerably. The soil was not nearly as rich. There was a large Black population along the road; there were banana trees again but the land was not heavily worked. It seemed very similar to the "mato" or countryside in parts of Brazil. There was some coffee, some yucca and some jute. We ran into heavy clouds as we entered the mountains. All was still totally green, not with the high sierra turf as in the "cordillera" down from Bogotá, but with vegetation. After several stops we rolled into Popayán with many vendors rushing the bus selling breads, meat and fruit. A Guambiano Indian boy got on and it appeared to be his first bus ride (the Guambianos enter the story later). There had been vomiting by children on the bus since Girardot.

POPAYÁN

This city is famous in Colombia as a regional university city. Our first impression was that it was very busy and fairly large. At first glance it did not seem to be as neat in appearance as Santa Fé de Antioquia, but it grows on you.

There is a large regional university here and it is linked to a rarity in 19th century Latin America: science and scientific research. The scientist and professor Caldas is the best known, and there is a plaza with customary statue dedicated to him. There were many students about and it reminded me a bit of Ouro Preto in Brazil.

The Monastery Hotel, Popayán

Keah at the Monastery Hotel, Popayán

Wooden Beams through Window, Monastery Hotel

We went immediately to the "Monasterio," now converted into one of the most interesting hotels in town, but alas there was no place at the inn; all the rooms were booked for a medical convention. And the hotel management was a bit surly about it; is this the future for us in Colombia? The Monastery has bricked floors throughout, flowers, arches everywhere, and the rooms which were the former tiny cells of the monks. It is all in stark white with brick floors in the rooms and windows and balconies of carved wood (the Colombian colonial trademark). It was the monastery of the Franciscans from 1570 to 1573 and later became the "Colegio de Misiones de Nuestra Señora de las Gracias" until 1863. Time passed and it evolved into a government barracks and office for local government officials and finally a hotel.

The buildings in Popayán all seemed to be colonial in style; the streets were narrow and there were row houses to the side. The main plaza was large and delightful, but the quiet atmosphere of Santa Fé de Antioquia was missing. We stayed at a modest hotel, not our choice, "Los Balcones," but went often to the "Monasterio" for drinks or coffee and were able to enjoy its beauty. Our first lunch in Popayán was at Restaurante Parma with Italian food, an odd pizza and thick steak, more like a ham slice in U.S. packaging. There were many Guambiano Indians in town, and I wrote, "They are the friendliest people we have met yet on this bus trip." As mentioned earlier, the central plaza is named after Caldas, evidently one of the few true men of science that Latin America produced through the 19th century.

LOOKING FOR THE COLONIAL HERITAGE IN POPAYÁN

THE CATHEDRAL

The cathedral dates from 1856 (there were earthquakes in this part of Colombia, thus this is a rebuilt version) and is of Doric style, neo-classic that is. The tabernacle was entirely silver, and the famous monstrance ("custodia") of pure gold and precious stones is in the vault of the Banco Popular, and for a good reason. They can no longer keep the valuable items in the churches in this country because of thievery. One must search out local bank vaults to see these treasures. But the richness and extravagance of the colonial church becomes evident in the vaults. It also gives thought to the Liberalism of 19th century Latin America and the general belief and complaint as to the riches of the Catholic Church. The image that is best known in this cathedral is the "Jesus Sentado," the "Seated Jesus," that is carried in the Holy Week processions.

LA TORRE DEL RELOJ

This is the central watch tower sporting the coat of arms given to Popayán by no less than King Carlos V, the Hapsburg of Spain's Golden Age. The Hapsburg coat of arms throughout the Spanish world is the double eagle—"el Águila Bicéfala."

Pulpit of the Church of San Francisco, Popayán

IGLESIA DE SAN FRANCISCO

This repaired church survived the earthquake. Originally built in 1788, it is in the Baroque style of Nueva Granada and is known for its gold and silver bell, "The Voice of Popayán." Devastating damage took place to this church and others in Popayán a year or two after our visit. The pulpit was impressive, one of the most unusual in the country: of carved wood, painted in gold, baroque in the style of the School of Quito, ornamental to the point of busyness.

THE MUSEUM OF SACRED ART

The building is connected to the Church of San Francisco. It had mummified monks, carved statues of many saints, very rich vestments of the colonial period and several famous religious paintings of Colombia, including one of Santa Bárbara, another "El Niño de la Espina" and "La Última Cena." There were virgins with wigs and brilliantly colored clothing provided by nuns from convents in Spain, gold chalices, tiaras and crowns of gold and silver with precious stones.

Monstrance of Gold, "Custodia de Oro," Popayán

As mentioned, the most famous item, the famous Monstrance of Gold (the receptacle which holds the Eucharist during processions) with its Double Eagle from the Austrian Crown of the Hapsburgs is in the Banco da la República of Popayán and is only taken out under guard during the Holy Week procession. One last impressive item was a Christ crucified on a huge silver cross.

THE MUSEUM OF COLONIAL ART

House-Museum of Guillermo de Valencia, Popayán

The owner of the former mansion, now museum, was a cousin of Guillermo Valencia, a Colombian poet of the Latin American Modernist Movement and eventual president of Colombia. An aside: I did a graduate seminar paper on him at Saint Louis University on a "thrilling poem" (pardon the sarcasm) called "The Camels" ["Los Camellos"] and as I said in "Coming of Age with the Jesuits," after handing in the paper it was suggested I leave the program by the professor of the course. Fortunately that did not happen. Blame the poet or the camels.

THE HUMILLADERO BRIDGE

Humilladero Bridge, Popayán

This is another local landmark from colonial days, a wide bridge with arches of stone. In centuries past supposedly only the aristocrats could use the bridge; the peons had to ford the small stream beneath. While there we were introduced by a local policeman to a local fruit, "chonta dura," which reminded me of salty sweet potato. We were given to understand by him that the bridge in modern days has become a hangout for marijuana smokers and other such shenanigans.

LA IGLESIA DE LA COMPANIA.

The former church of the Jesuits is today called San José; recall once again the Jesuits were thrown out of all Portuguese and Spanish possessions in 1767. Their properties were confiscated by the State or awarded to other orders. The church was very poor in appearance and seemed badly cared for. A rosary is said very afternoon before mass.

"UMA PEQUEÑA SALIDA:" POPAYÁN TO SILVIA AND THE GUAMBIANO INDIANS

We were up at the crack of dawn for a forty minute bus ride to the tiny town of Piandamo, arriving under a grey, cold sky with threatening rain. There were not enough people waiting for the taxi to Silvia at the crossroads at Piandamo so we waited until enough could pool for the ride. It is a crossroads town, and jeeps and beat up old cars are used for the trip to Silvia (why there was no bus escapes me, especially on market day). We began a rather steep climb and we were soon above the clouds and it became quite cold. The chauffer never took the car out of third gear. Green pastures were to the side of the road, but there was little under cultivation. The trip took thirty-five minutes and there were several mud slides along the way.

We arrived together with driving rain in Silvia. There was a large Indian market with all manner of articles for tourists and Indians coming into town for the day. Market booths were replete with multi-colored woolen blankets and a large selection of "ruanas." Inside the market were vegetables of all kinds, local fruits, breads, clothing, hardware for the house, machetes and articles of leather. Mud was everywhere and there was an incredible smell from the wetness.

Guambiano Indians in the Plaza of Silvia

The Guambiano Indians who live in the surrounding rural area around Silvia, according to one view, are extremely independent. In this highly conservative part of Colombia they traditionally vote with the liberal party. The manner of dress is unique and colorful, much different than what we had seen in Guatemala in Central America. Women wore a black skirt trimmed in red, colored blouse and a "ruana" or "chal" of brilliant blue with a red border. They wore a coffee-colored felt hat which looked like a man's hat. And they carried on their back a bag which included goods from market or perhaps a baby. Almost all the ladies had large quantities of white beads around their neck. They were generally wearing colored tennis shoes, many in the high topped style we used to wear in grade school in the 1940s and 1950s in Kansas. I never saw one of the ladies doing nothing: while they walk or speak they were preparing thread out of yarn using a rapid, nervous motion of the hands. And their facial features were unlike natives in the U.S. or in Meso-America, as it were, a bit more . . . what? European? Just a coincidence I am sure.

The men wore a kind of blue-purple skirt, shirt and a stylized black "ruana" and a hat of the same style as the women. Many wore high topped, unlaced tennis shoes or rubber or plastic galoshes.

They were scattered in groups throughout the plaza, the women weaving their thread or just looking around.

There was an unusual character outside the market; I'll call him a "carny" man, a "ladino" type with some snakes in a box and two scruffy monkeys. He was "ugly," motley and with a microphone and was selling popular remedies to the Indians. Another "mestizo" type with no teeth walked around with a box in which he placed a globe, a sort of "crystal ball" with a shrunken head inside the globe. He carried many envelopes with a blue hand stamped on one side. For two pesos he would slide the envelope under the globe and thus determine the horoscope (or fortune) of the customer. He seemed to be a good talker and con-man; while we watched he took in a lot of cash. To his side was a short of shaman with a feathered headdress and a small table with herbs, potions and leaflets with prayers on them.

Otavalo Indian in White with Shawls for Sale

Otavalo Indian in Black "Ruana" Counting the Proceeds

For the first time, but far from the last, we encountered the traveling vendors of woolen articles, "ruanas," "chales" and the like, the Otavalo Indians from across the border in Ecuador. They wore loose, white "pantalones," a white shirt, their hair in braids and a felt hat on their head. There is much more to tell about them later. We bought some "escharpes," scarves, and shawls, all pure wool and richly woven. They were much finer than those I had seen in places in Peru or Mexico.

After the market we went to the "Hotel de Turismo" but it turned out to be a bit much for our budget. So we had the noon meal in a "pensión" called "Residencia la Parilla." It was literally full of hippies, some of whom were talking about drugs. The magic mushrooms are particularly well-known in the region, and many of the hippies were from the Key West area. Most were fairly badly dressed, many with beards, in short, the 60s scene. Curiously enough, a Colombian in the inn thought we were English because all the Americans had the appearance of hippies. The "almuerzo" was tasty with fruit salad, beef, rice, fried potatoes and fried bananas, 22 pesos for the two of us.

End of the Market Day, Guambiano Indians, Silvia

Countryside Outside of Silvia with Guambiano Indians

On the outskirts of town there is a very fast running river; all around it are green fields and pasture land with many horses and burros. These pastures rise up into fairly large hills on the outskirts of town.

It continued to pour down rain so we left town early in a taxi for Popayán. It broke down once, but the driver was able to fix something and we moved on. There were many broken down vehicles along the highway "home."

POPAYÁN ONCE AGAIN

After a siesta after the long day in Silvia we walked about the town and purchased some fine, wood burned plaques. There was a student demonstration in the streets, the leader with a microphone with many shouts of "viva" and "abajo." What I could understand is that they wanted to throw some professors out of the Universidad del Cauca.

The Bakeries in Popayán. There was an incredible variety of good things to eat. Our favorite was a "pan de coco," cocoanut bread the likes of which we have never found elsewhere in Latin America. We enjoyed bags of popcorn bought on the street and later entered a bar for "Poker" Beer and later, ice cream. It was raining cats and dogs so we retired early to the "pension" for rest and writing these notes.

The Next Day.

There was another student manifestation this morning.

We did a "paseo" through the north part of Popayán, up the hill to the Way of the Cross or "Vía Crucis" and the Bethlehem Chapel, "Capilla de Belén." The Way of the Cross is pretty with large stone sculptures of the stations, cobblestone walkways, many flowers and all was extremely green with luxurious vegetation. The Chapel is new since the earthquake destroyed the original. Its main statue the "Ecce Homo" is in the Basilica. The view of the city from above was impressive: titled roofs, houses, greenery, and the airport in the distance. A local landmark, the Liquor Distillery or "Fábrica de Licores," is in open country to the north and east.

We walked along the Parque de la Mosquera along the Río Molino and noticed the daffodils and the marijuana smokers and the "Árbol de Mayo" with bright orange flowers. I think this is the same as the "Árbol del Casamiento" in Central America.

Lunch was a favorite, "pollo al horno," delicious, plentiful and about 85 cents U.S. Then came an elaborate procedure for cashinig a traveler's check.

That night.

We had dinner and then attended a folk music concert in the "Paraninfo Caldas" Hall at the Universidad del Cauca. The hall featured a great mural by Efraín Martínez, "A History of Popayán," and on the wall was the text of "A Popayán," the poem by Guillermo Valencia. The music was excellent with fine guitar work and singing and the solo singer with ultra-dramatic operatic type gestures, "muy latino." There was a student demonstration in the hall at the end of the concert, a bit unsettling but no problem.

The Next Day—Conversations with a Colombia Student

We enjoyed a long conversation with student Jorge Cortés, majoring in accounting and from Bogotá. We spoke of Socialism, the student manifestations, and religion and church in Colombia. He believed the latter was linked to the oligarchy and the poverty (85 per cent of the people earn $50 U.S. or less per month, 1500 pesos, 30 to the dollar at this point). There is a national monopoly by the agricultural corporations. He says three families control the entire production of sugar and sugar cane in the Valle del Cauca. Two kilos of sugar in Popayán cost 35 cents U.S., in the U.S. about $2.45. We also spoke of Latin hospitality. Curious: he mentioned that he had seen us in Popayán and three times had wanted to get up the courage to speak to us. Musing: I perhaps am a slow learner, or not. Oftentimes the seeming unfriendliness I encounter in Latin America is not unfriendliness at all but shyness perhaps brought on by the stereotype of the American who says he knows Spanish/Portuguese and knows nothing of the countries. Remember to make the first move!

We went to a bank surrounded by soldiers with sub-machine guns where we exchanged yet another travelers' check, and then to the bus station to buy the ticket for tomorrow's journey to San Agustín. Of note in the bank was the man weighing, exchanging and then selling loose gold. There was time for a final trip to the market. Once again we saw the same men from Otavalo who had sold goods in the market at Silvia and were now doing the same in Popayán. We would encounter these "the most capitalistic of South American Indians" later on in Bogotá, Cartagena and even San Andrés Island in the Caribbean. (We were told they sell in Miami and New York City as well.) And the herb salesman was there as well selling sulphur for "moles on the skin," "manchas en la piel."

We went to the Hotel Monasterio for a break, then to the main plaza and a café. While resting in the plaza we killed time watching men paint the Basilica (the exterior painting of buildings is always interesting in Latin America); they were on bamboo scaffolding and a young boy was lying down on the roof and precariously hanging over the edge to paint.

Scene in the Park.

There were several Guambiano Indians, little girls taking photos and flirting, and a little boy making fun of a beggar.

We walked up the hill once again to the church of "La Hermita" (the Hermitage), the oldest of Popayán. It had a thatch roof, was beautiful but very simple. Then we walked through a very small but exclusive residential area that was gorgeous. That evening for the first time it did not rain and there was a pretty sunset, very pleasant but cool temperature, no pollution—a very pretty way to end our stay in Popayán.

JOURNEY TO THE ARCHEOLOGICAL SITE OF SAN AGUSTÍN

We got up at three a.m. and walked in pitch darkness and rain down to the very modest and small bus station. There were U.S. hippies standing around, some recently arrived from San Agustín with passports and documents robbed on the way. The bus line, by the way, to San Agustín was called "La Muerte Amarilla" ("Yellow Death"), a reference either to its yellow color or its reputation. At early dawn and by now high in the Andes, we passed through a strange, almost surreal zone: there was heavy rain, fog, and everything was covered with a kind of mossy mildew. It reminded me of a scene from a film of pre-historic times (dinosaurs, swamps, fog, rain), a kind of "nether-world." There was a tiny bus stop on top of the "cordillera" with a café; it was filthy and extremely poor. The coffee was served in bowls, and one saw coal or coals from wood for the cooking.

We later passed through a humid region but now with grass pasture like the savannah near Bogotá. Then we passed through a large valley with a very fast running, rough river, everything seemingly in larger than life dimension. There were dozens of "May Trees" ("Árboles de Mayo") in this area called La Plata. The next zone had banana and coffee trees in abundance, all green and lush. Then the road, such as it was, finally straightened out in a place called Pitalito, no longer the meandering roads of the Andes. Then a little before San Agustín we passed through a region along the Magdalena River, worse than "El Tapón" between southern Mexico and northern Guatemala, a place I described in "Coming of Age with the Jesuits." El Tapón was a pass along the border. Here from on top of the "cordillera," way down below was the river, the road was up on a ledge to the left; it was in horrible shape with big holes and one huge mud slide. The bus stopped, the driver got out checking things out and then we forged ahead!

ARRIVAL IN SAN AGUSTÍN

Mark Outside the Country Hotel, San Agustín

The town itself seemed quite small to me with few paved or cobblestoned streets. We stayed in the only lodging, the Hotel Yalconia with no hot water but with a beautiful view of plants of all types, orchids and "chupa-flores" or hummingbirds. All was green and lush. Hippies on the very bus in which we crossed the Andes were robbed during the bus ride. We were always cautious, hanging on to documents, billfolds and purses for dear life. There were never any problems but it was not exactly relaxing at times.

Party at the Hotel.

Last night was fun. A group of school age kids from Bogotá were at the hotel and they requested some local music. A trio showed up with drums ("tambores"), flutes ("flautas"), and a very folkloric, country, simple music was played. It reminded me of the "Música Pindín" with sound box from

Panamá. With all the partying ("festejo") and noise I later somehow succeeded in sleeping over eleven hours! It was exhaustion from the previous day's journey over the Andes from Popayán.

SAN AGUSTÍN'S PRE-COLOMBIAN CULTURE

San Agustín is the most important archeological site in Colombia. The civilization was purported to be of Pre-Incan time. There one finds hundreds of monolithic statues, some of unusually large height, ceremonial fountains, tombs covered with stone slabs, and sarcophagi within. It was a religious site frequented by many tribes of the region and its main emphasis seemed to be a burial place. First notice of the site was in 1756, but it was not until the 20th century that excavation and study of the site seriously began. But the origins and real story of this civilization are still much clouded in the mysteries of time past.

Well rested, up at eight after a good breakfast of bread, butter, marmalade, eggs, ham and coffee, we were fortified for a walk to the Parque Arqueológico, a distance of about three or four kilometers. On the way there were green pastures, lots of beautiful birds and a country atmosphere (how different from the sites in the Yucatán with thousands of tourists, a scene we would see one year later). It is the small places that I loved most in Colombia, far from the large cities, and there were many of them.

San Agustín Idol

San Agustín Idol

We proceeded on to the Park and what they call "Mesitas ABC." There were beautiful orchids all about in the trees and of course the statues or monuments themselves from the San Agustín culture. While at the park we met some young Americans from the Peace Corps contingent in Ibagüé. "Mesita A" had statues of "The sun, the eagle, the warrior, the goddess of maternity and "Bird foot" ("el sol, el águila, el guerrero, la diosa de la maternidad, y "ave patas.") "Mesita C" had "The Moon" ("La luna)," etc. The forest was full of mosquitoes, incredible tropical vegetation, orchids and nearby, a very poor, tiny museum.

THE HOTEL OSOGUAIC AND THE MAGIC MUSHROOMS

On a return walk to our hotel at the edge of town we went by the Hotel Osoguaic, a very picturesque place. The owner was a German lady with a wig, speaking very bad Spanish and of course with a foreign accent (one always thinks of Nazi refugees in the midst of the jungle, recent cases in Argentina, Brazil and Paraguay in point). There was a beautiful view from the hotel down to the "pueblo" and the mountains in the background.

Here we met the smiling hippy who collected and ate "magic mushrooms" ("hongos mágicos"). He was stoned and happy, evidenced by a permanent shit-eating grin across his face. He admitted to eating from 50 to 75 mushrooms per day for the psilocybin in them. He said he lived on a little farm ("finca") about 45 minutes from there; he was from Key West where he has a health food store. Perhaps he was gathering "health food" for this enterprise. He told of an encounter with the police and of being dragged down to the station for possible violations. He reported he just played a few songs on his trusty guitar from the "Grateful Dead" and all was "cool." He maintained he was able to produce good vibrations with that ole' guitar and never had any problems. He also told of a taxi trip to Popayán costing 240 pesos and eight hours of travel, the ostensive purpose to get hashish. He said the magic mushrooms actually grow out of cow pies, and that it indeed was a humbling, close to the earth experience in picking them! He said they were great in Hungarian "goulash" or Argentine "churrasco." Many other hippies were in the area, renting small houses from the locals.

We returned to our hotel and there was heavy rain most of the night, but with a resulting atmosphere in the country of pure air and absolute blackness in the heavens. Lights went out in the modest hotel, but there was a long conversation with the tourist agency group from Medellín "irrigated" by lots of "aguardiente," the licorice flavored "Anís" of Colombia.

At one point we had a conversation with the Peace Corps kids from Medellín; all work for "Bienestar Familiar." Query: is this family planning? Each earns 60$ per month.

RETURN TO THE ARCHEOLOGICAL PARK

The return was beautiful; there were very few visitors, and a mysterious atmosphere seemed to envelop the place, particularly when one thinks of the idols and statues amidst luxurious tropical vegetation. It was a good idea of the Colombian government to make the Park entrance fee low enough so the common people ("pueblo") can afford to see it.

The time arrived for a trip to "The High Rocky Place" ("Alto de las Piedras") to see more idols. We hired a taxi chauffeured by a certain Eduardo and were accompanied by the Peace Corps crowd. He drove through a high pass above the Magdalena River with irrigated, terraced crops on the side of the hills. Then we proceeded up through the tiny town of San José de Isnos to the site—Alto de las Piedras. The idols were called "The Warrior and the Double I" (El Guerrero y el Doble Yo), the latter a serpent with a man's face and a mother with a child. Then we went back to the pueblo of San José with a stop at the local market. Afterwards there were even more idols at another section of the "Alto:" "The fisherman, the guard with arrows" ("el pescador, el vigilán con las flechas,") a sarcophagus with "sleeves," and "the rat, the noble, and the crocodiles" ("el ratón, el noble, y los cocodrilos.")

MASS IN SAN AGUSTÍN

It was a very simple, country church. During mass with an absolutely full crowd, the men sat on one side of the aisle, women on the other. Most of the attendees were Indian. Men were dressed in white "ruanas" with stripes. For a change the sermon was in very clear Spanish. Few received communion.

RETURN TO THE HOTEL

Finally, there was a bath with hot water that night in the hotel. While writing these notes we heard the folk band with flute and drums; again there was a fair quantity of "Anís" with the girls from the tourist agencies from Medellín, Manizales, and Pereira, a good time for all.

The Next Day. Life in San Agustín

We went to town where we bought bus tickets for the trip to Girardot tomorrow. Then we went to the market with its market smells of vegetables, chickens and turkeys. With the rain, all was muddy. We changed money at the "Caja Agraria Nacional," a rural farm bank full of people from the countryside ("campesinos"). Then it was back to the Hotel Osoguaico for "almuerzo," steak with rice, and papas. While we ate we watched a campesino cutting cane for his animals near the hotel; all were thin and they looked like they needed the nourishment. We got to know the German owner a bit; she had a huge garden where she grew many of the vegetables served in the hotel. Among the produce was coffee beans drying in the sun. The coffee is grown, picked, toasted and ground right here. The atmosphere in her inn was very interesting, like a hostel in Europe I surmise.

Keah on Horseback, Pueblo de San Agustín

OUTING ON HORSEBACK

We did another "paseo" but this time on horseback beginning down through the "pueblo" and then up into the hills to a place they call the "Tableland" ("Tablado") where there were five more idols in an open field. It took one and one-half hours and that was long enough. Both of us were saddle-sore. Spunky horses they were, and it was a neat feeling riding down into the "pueblo," right out of an old western movie. One noticed the horse farts ("Las gaseosas de los caballos")."

SUMMARY OF SAN AGUSTÍN

So the visit to San Agustín came to an end. We thoroughly enjoyed the little town and the tranquility of the place, being able to speak freely to people, even strangers, without the fear of pickpockets, thieves, etc. as in the cities. Highlights were the friendliness of the people, the immense beauty of the spot, the park and the archeological site, the comfort of our Hotel Yanconia and the entertaining atmosphere of the Hotel Osoguaico.

We did not like the oppressive humidity, the flies and many of the hippies. Some sundry scenes were: black "toros" fighting in the pastures, a man walking with long stalks of bananas, and another man on horseback who told me all about the business of buying and selling horses in the area.

There was a patio in town where men gathered and played a sort of "horseshoe" game; it involved a wooden ball, stacks of mud balls pitched to hit said wooden ball, obviously a game for poor people. Conversations with the players revealed men who complained of the national government and the lack of progress in this area.

There was a camping area nearby where you can park your car for 20 pesos (one dollar is 30 pesos), and the natives will rent you a little country shack and a horse for 15 days or a month.

RETURN TO GIRARDOT

We awakened to cloudy, rainy skies, a good day to leave. On the way to the bus station we were "corralled" by a little old lady, a "church lady" ("beata") type who complained of everything and showed us her "pensión" where you can sleep and eat for 80 pesos.

The bus was the "milk route," stopping absolutely everywhere which was all right with us because we saw more. I noted the accelerator on the bus was made of silver colored steel and was in the form of a bare human foot. You don't see that every day. Everything went well until we reached the area of the slides. All traffic stopped and we heard "There's no way through" ("No hay paso"). The bus waited for about four hours while a dozer worked on the slide and cleared a truck jackknifed in the road. Once allowed to pass, it took our driver about ten minutes to get through the scary area, worse as I said than the Tapón in Guatemala. It turns out traffic was interrupted in all the southern part of the country with the recent rains and slides. We followed the Magdalena River, gradually dropping from the Andes to a valley near Neiva and rice country. At the end of the day we arrived to Giradot and Linda Buller's house to a U.S. nicety—cinnamon rolls.

THE LEPER COLONY OF ÁGUA DE DIOS

The next p.m. we traveled to the Água de Dios Leper Colony, ostensibly to see the shoe factory Linda Buller had started for the lepers. It was with no little trepidation that we made the trip; our knowledge of leprosy was limited to scenes from the Bible and vague memories from a film on a Leper colony in Hawaii. The main concern was how does one contract leprosy?

The trip did open my eyes to the disease, and it was the first time (only time, none since) I had ever been to a colony. Most of the lepers' feet were partially or totally deformed, so the trick is to make individual molds of each person's foot and make a custom shoe. Foam rubber must be used on the inside so the shoes will be molded to the form of the foot. The work was of the highest quality. One sees the molds, the samples and the finished shoes in the shop.

The Colombian government is beginning to see the good work that has been done and for the first time sees the possibilities of actually trying to help the lepers instead of ignoring or isolating them. It all began with one man's work in Trinidad, then Linda's trip to Africa where she visited colonies. She then received the financial seed money from the Presbyterian Church in the United States (thus the ties to the Emerys) and finally the financial aid of the Malaria and Leprosy Section of the Colombian national government. It was interesting to see her perspective: getting the Colombian employees in the colony to actually work, including the "lazy secretary with the skimpy clothes." One Herr Gerhardt Goldman, a German who came to work with Linda after years of working with lepers in Uganda had his own story. He had to leave Uganda because of the dictator Idi Amin. There was a long problem with the Colombian bureaucracy in order to get his work visa and other necessary working papers. But all worked out.

A weather report: the weather is still rainy; yesterday there was hail in Bogotá. The road to Água de Dios followed lots of level ground planted in cotton, sesame, and we saw a lot of Brahma stock. The houses were country huts: stick and mud wattle with thatch roofs.

The problem of leprosy is complicated. There are about 4000 lepers in this colony or town with one large hospital administered by Dutch personnel with in-patient and out-patient care. Leprosy is probably contagious only over an extended period of physical contact. Many in the same family do not get it, and there is no danger of contagion to people like doctors, nurses like Linda, etc. There is less stigma to the disease than in the past. We were mightily impressed with the courage of these caregivers, of the charity, religious, Godly work. An aside on leprosy: Linda explained that deformed hands and feet are not the problems themselves, but the fact that the nerve endings are destroyed by the disease and there is no feeling. Thus, toes and feet are injured, bleed, and get infected, and hands and fingers are burned by cigarettes. The idea is to protect both from further injury.

We also visited the hospital; I recall beds and sectors protected by high mosquito nets. One unsettling fact was we were told the "incubation" period for leprosy is up to seven years after contact, notwithstanding the information above. The key word to the above item is "probably."

Next Day in Girardot

We were again at the market, a walk to downtown and home for rest and writing. The heat is extreme with high humidity. We tried to walk to the bridge over the Magdalena River but were warned to be careful of the "rateros" or thieves. So once again we were on edge. We did manage to drink the coldest beer yet in Colombia.

NATIONAL POLITICS AND NEWS

The big news is that there is a newly elected female governor of one of the departments of Colombia whose mandate was vetoed by the bishops of the Catholic Church because she is divorced and married anew in a civil ceremony outside the church. In Colombia it is a scandal, almost a small Watergate. Anti-clericalism is everywhere, this due to the overwhelming power of the old church. The lady had an emotional encounter with her former husband outside the gubernatorial palace. Due to an old concordat between Colombia and the Vatican, there is no legal divorce in this country (circa 1975). So many persons travel to Venezuela to get the "$2000 special," combining divorce and vacation. I wondered if the vacation came first or last. And do they do separate bedrooms?

MUSING IN COLOMBIA

I am thinking today of all we have seen so far, approximately one-half way through our trip. It is difficult to see how many of the Colombians survive here; there is so much misery, poverty, and lack of concern by those with resources for those without. Life becomes cheap and fragile; there is danger on a daily basis to even get on a bus or walk down certain streets. Houses are locked "a diez llaves" ("with ten keys"). Such conditions are of course not restricted to Colombia, but we had not experienced them to this point in Tempe, Arizona. News is of robberies, street theft and the great precautions one must take in Colombia. An aside: in the 1980s in Brazil, especially in Rio and São Paulo, it is exactly the same. Colombia was just ahead of its time.

PART III. BOGOTÁ AND BEYOND: TRIP TO THE NORTH AND HISTORIC BOYACÁ STATE

THE RETURN TO BOGOTÁ

We returned via Autobuses Fusa, the milk route again with all kinds of stops. (You have to remember to ask for a "directo.") With the stops in all kinds of towns, we had to keep an eye on the suitcases in the racks above us in case of problems. Some were placed on the floor by the driver so each time the bus stopped we had to check on them. It made for a nervous trip, but we never were robbed!

For the first time we were greeted in Bogotá with blue skies and a bit of warmth. We returned to the Emerys where we met Jim's older brother John for the first time, recently arrived from Puerto Rico. With a Harvard MBA in hand, he is going to work for Cessna in the Andean countries. He seemed a good person, very similar to Jim, gentle and friendly.

TOURISM TO MONSERRATE

The next day we took the "teleférico" or cable car up Monserrate Mountain. From the top you can see all of Bogotá, even with a bit of clouds or fog: the south industrial zone, the colonial or old city of the center with its tiled roofs, the downtown with the skyscrapers, the Avianca Building, Bolívar Plaza with the Cathedral, the Church of San Francisco, and the hotel zone with the Tequendama and the Hilton. In the north zone, far off, you could see the airport and mountains in the distance. We visited the Chapel of Monserrate with the image of the reclining Jesus. On the other side of the mountains one could see eucalyptus trees, poplars and a kind of pine.

The outing to Monserrate was followed by the famous, in those parts, "Quinta de Bolívar" at the foot of the mountain. This was the Bolívar home and garden, a place given to him after 1820 and the victorious battle for independence. There were beautiful gardens, flowers, pools, fountains and a one-story house, open and colonial in style. The furniture was colonial of course, and there were many paintings of him, his generals, and his concubine Manuela Sáens who "reigned" with him. According to the guide book much of the original furniture had been replaced, the originals stolen by "subversives." Not as pleasant as it could have been with such reminders.

From the Quinta we went to the Universidad de los Andes on a rise before the mountains. They tell us the area in the back of the university is dangerous, a poor area known for black market emeralds, but the view of the city from there is pretty. So what to do? I had an appointment with Charlotte Samper the dean and we discussed a possible ASU summer school with them. But Charlotte had a more interesting offer: why don't you come to Bogotá and the Universidad and teach Portuguese? It seems there was some demand and of course a scarcity of professors of the same in Colombia. I pondered the matter for a bit, but "naaah."

THE DORA LUZ EPISODE ONCE AGAIN

The Catholic bishops continue to complain about the new governess: she has accepted the job. The bishops will not withdraw their veto and the country is faced with a dilemma.

A SOCIAL MOMENT AT THE EMERYS

That night we all went to the home of Gerhard and Inge Goldman with their guests from New Jersey, the gentleman an employee of Chase Manhattan Bank. The Goldmans have extensive experience in Pakistan, Uganda and now Colombia with the Leprosy Control Mission. They are both trained nurses, trained to diagnose leprosy which is done by a testing of the arms, hands and feet. They talked of many things—the "papeleo" or red-tape in Colombia even in trying to mail a package in the post, for visas to leave the country, of Colombian politics, the conflicts with the "guerrillas" in the countryside, the Socialist labor unions—in short what is going on there and if there really is any plan for progress. I, strangely enough, listened a lot and talked little. There was a nice dinner of steak a la fondue, salad, dessert and wine. I played a class guitar made by a German in Bogotá.

SUNDAY SCENE IN BOGOTÁ

We got up late and took a bus to mass at the Iglesia de San Diego near the Tequendama Hotel; the church had a side altar with an image of the Virgen, very pretty with a half-moon under her feet. We walked all the way home, about forty minutes, seeing TV artists along the way doing a parade for charity. The walk was, for a change in Bogotá, very tranquil and beautiful. There were children roller skating, people walking their dogs, many on a "paseo" after mass. The homes in this sector are old, many of European style; they seemed English or Swiss. There were small stores or "tiendas," cigarette shops and cafés on the corners. It reminded me a bit of the streets of Leblon in Rio, minus the beach of course.

A Note on Transportation in Bogotá in 1975

The taxis were of all descriptions, generally old "cucarachas," but we saw some Chevies and Fords of 1959-1964 vintage and many Renaults.

There seemed to be dozens of bus companies. One type of bus was similar to a VW Van, old, dirty, always full of people. These were like the "peseros" in Mexico City. And there were many "busetas," (careful with this word when Brazilians present!) and a lot of newer ones that were always full. But the most common were those that looked like U.S. school buses. And there were a few

Greyhound types as in the U.S. It was a bit strange to see the latter with a well-dressed, uniformed driver with a tie.

For what it is worth, and it's not worth much, there is an anecdote in my notes. This is pure "folklore" and speculative folklore at that. Someone told us that the reason many do not seat themselves immediately in the bus when a seat becomes open, is that they are letting it "rest." The person said such hesitant passengers fear venereal disease or possible pregnancy. I have no further information on who exactly said this or which passengers he had in mind. Perhaps we were hallucinating from the long conversation with Mr. Mushroom Man.

A Note on the Weather in Bogotá

During our stay a clear and transparent day was rare, but when it came it was worth it because of the view of the beautiful mountains that surround the city. From Monserrate you can see for miles. But generally there was a haze of natural fogginess or clouds from the mountains and or contamination. When it rains it is cool and a bit uncomfortable. The best attire as a tourist is a long sleeved shirt and a "ruana" on top; you can let the latter fall naturally or double over the shoulder when it is a bit warmer. And an umbrella never hurts either.

State of the Country

The Emerys tell us the recession in the U.S. has not affected Colombia that much yet. There is 15-20 per cent annual inflation, but that is normal. There was lots of construction, industrialization and mining. Agriculture is varied, not at all dependent on one crop (like the old days of coffee).

TUNJA AND BOYACÁ STATE

We took the "Rápido Duitama" out of north Bogotá en route to Tunja, "rápido" being an understatement. It was a fine bus, almost luxury in comparison to what we have seen so far; they even give you candy before the start of the trip! The bus passed through the "sabana de Bogotá," that is, green grassy plains with many cattle ranches on level ground. Then there was a change to wheat and barley farms, some hilly and terraced; the climate here is dryer. We passed from the latifundary zone, that is, the large haciendas, to the "mini-fundio" area where there are many small fields and farms of potatoes and the land was tilled in many instances by plows pulled by oxen. They plant on the sides of the hills and it all is very picturesque. The people seemed poor in appearance but the countryside is very pretty with very deep valleys cultivated on the sides. This is all in Colombia's Boyacá State.

The Bridge at Boyacá

Monument at the Bridge of Boyacá

We passed the famous "Puente de Boyacá" or Boyacá Bridge where Bolívar defeated the Spaniards in a decisive battle in the campaign for Independence on August 7, 1819; the previous day he had taken the city of Tunja from the Spanish loyalists. In this final battle with the help of an English legion, the only professional soldiers in his force, he lost only 13 men with 53 wounded while capturing 1600 enlisted men and 39 Spanish officers. Upon hearing the news of this defeat at the Bridge of Boyacá the Spanish Viceroy Samao fled, leaving one half million pesos in his haste.

ARRIVAL IN TUNJA AND THE SEARCH FOR ITS COLONIAL HERITAGE

So we arrived at Tunja whose surroundings seemed very dry; the terrain was hilly with fields of potatoes and there was lots of wind and it was cold. It was 13 degrees centigrade (in the 40s F) when we arrived.

Tunja was founded in 1539 by Gonzalo Suárez Rendón and was the previous capital of the Chibcha Indians. General Suárez Rendón in turn served under Jiménez de Quesada, the principal Spanish Conquistador of Colombia and founder of Bogotá. Suárez Rendón hung the last Chibcha king and his vassals in the Plaza of Tunja.

The city has been compared to Toledo in Spain for its geography, climate, and architecture. The old city is full of mansions with wooden balconies, patios, and flowers; churches and cloisters, and the main buildings with coats of arms displayed above large porticos. The city declared itself independent from Spain in 1811 by the "Junta para la Independencia" and went under the aegis of Bolívar in 1812. Actual independence came six years later.

Plaza de Tunja with School Children, Cathedral and Statue of Bolívar

Stone Doorway, "Pórtico," in the Plaza de Tunja

THE CENTRAL PLAZA

We walked to the central plaza which was huge and cobblestoned. The visitor is impressed with its size, the huge statue of Bolívar, the colonial houses on all sides with wooden balconies, large wooden, carved doors or "portadas," and the Cathedral on one side of the plaza. The central city plan of the Spaniards is much the same all over Spanish America, but the regional tone is different. Peru seemed very different from Guatemala and Mexico, and Colombia from them.

There were difficulties in the quest to see colonial Tunja. We went to the main office of tourism and were told that Mondays and Tuesdays are lousy, you can't see anything, and that the most famous church, Santo Domingo, is closed for repairs. So we ended up with a visit to a third-stringer, the ole' Club Boyacá, former home of Don Jerónimo de Holguín, later to be mayor of Bogotá in 1582. The portico sported the usual coat of arms and the building was of Andalusian architectural style. Tradition has it that the Club offered a dance in the big salon on the second floor to the "Gran Libertador" on August 6, the night before the battle of the Bridge of Boyacá. Hmm. One wonders what shape the soldiers were in after the party? The Spaniards must have been feeling worse.

THE SAN FRANCISCO CHURCH.

An old priest took me by the shoulder and gave us the royal tour. Rather a sad figure (I borrowed from Cervantes to call him "the priest of the sad countenance" ("el padre de la triste figura"), he complained of the crises in the church since Vatican II, the lack of new vocations and the departure of many priests. "Somos muy pocos ahora." The convent was founded in 1550 but was in sad shape in 1975; the main church was built in 1572. The altar was different from anything we had seen in Colombia up to this point but was indeed impressive: it was of gold leaf, in Gothic style, and with an altar of "cedro nogal;" that seems contradictory; perhaps it was of cedar and walnut. The priest took us around on his "personal" tour and showed us many paintings. It was interesting to see a fellow restoring a "retablo" or altar, painting first in yellow and then with gold leaf.

THE DOMINICAN CONVENT.

Here we saw the remains of the church of Santo Domingo; the roof had fallen in and they want to restore the entire church. They need five million Colombian pesos and the government has given them only 800,000 so the restoration has been halted. The interior seemed to be entirely covered in gold and red and seemed very baroque in style. They have discovered the original stones of the original floor and paintings of St. Francis dating to 1594. The "Capilla del Rosario" dates from 1686. Ceiling paintings like those of the Casa de Don Juan de Vargas have also been discovered under recent coverings but have not been restored.

We were taken inside the convent where there are entire rooms full of articles taken from the main church, most half destroyed and in pieces. We saw the library with all the centuries of dust and literally worm-eaten books and many saints' images and paintings, i.e. the mother of St. Dominic with the dog and the candle and the famous vision, St. Dominic, the Wandering Jew, St. Thomas of Aquinas, the Reclining Jesus, the Nazarean. Before all this was a museum; today it is a "depósito" or warehouse.

Cathedral in the Plaza de Tunja

THE CATHEDRAL OF TUNJA.

It is on the main plaza and dates from 1569 to 1600. The style is Gothic with the pointed toral arch and the chapel of the "Mancipes" in Mudéjar style as is the roof of the Presbitério. The oil paintings are in the Renaissance style of the 16th century. The central altar is dressed in gold leaf, as is the sacristy ("sagrario,") the latter particularly shiny and very ostentatious. And there is also General Rondón's Chapel ("Capilla de Rendón,") beautiful, very old, of carved wood and with many small angels,("angelitos"). There are paintings by the Colombian master Vásquez y Ceballos, the Quiteño styled sculpture of a "Jesus Crucificado," and of course, the tomb of Rendón.

For some reason the next morning we returned to the Cathedral. We saw the sanctuary again, all in gold, perhaps "the most important of this style in Latin America," so says the guide book.

Then we revisited the "Capilla de los Mancipe" which is now an art museum with huge, Renaissance style paintings. The ceiling is in the Mudéjar style and there is an interesting picture of St. George with sword in hand cutting off a head.

The Capilla de Domingos Carmargo in the same church and done in the 16th century possessed a sort of 3D effect with large "azulejo" tiles, red planks and with gold leaf pieces nailed on to them, the figures depicted on the pieces with very heavy lines, like a woodcut; they seemed primitive perhaps with Indian motifs.

A LITERARY HIGHLIGHT: LA CASA DE DON JUAN DE CASTELLLANOS

Don Juan was a poet of the period; today the Casa is a shop with "Artesanías de Barne." On the ceiling there are frescos of the "Manierista" style, 16th century European, similar to those we saw in the Casa de Don Juan de Vargas in Tunja as well. The poet actually has a place in the anthologies of Latin American Literature; he wrote "Illustrious Men of the Indies." ("Varones Ilustres de Indias").

In the same vicinity is a tiny plaza called "La Plazoleta del Mono de la Pila," reconstructed, and they have a local legend telling something or other about the place as an important place of gossip in its era.

LA CASA DE DON JUAN DE VARGAS

This place houses a very impressive museum today. Don Juan was the eldest son of Don Diego de Vargas, "Gobernador General de la Nueva Granada" in 1564. The façade is of sculpted rock with his coat of arms; the interior has a brick floor. In the back is a beautiful patio with fountain and flowers, arches and columns, and the stable. From the second floor one sees the entire valley surrounding Tunja. The museum sports coats of arms of the times—sword and shield—a huge desk from Spain, a "caja forte" or strong box, for the mail ("correo"). The ceiling is famous, at least in Colombia, and depicts the Coat of Arms of Spain being lifted by "two savages." There are lions, jaguars, elephants and stylized Indians in the background.

The museum also had a coach for transporting the ladies of the times. In another salon there are more frescos but of a different theme—the fantastic. As well one sees the Vargas coat of arms, a shield with the Virgin Mary, Jesus, and Joseph. Griffins, fantastic animals, are also present. There is also religious art, statues, two huge doorways, one in Baroque style, another in Salomonic style, both ornate and with gold leaf. There is a tapestry from Jerusalem made of silver thread with the coat of arms of the "Caballeros del Santo Sepulcro," Knights of the Holy Sepulcher.

The bedroom had a brazier for coals to warm the room, a tiny bed, trunks for clothing, a marble lavoratory and paintings. The kitchen had a huge chimney, oven, smaller oven and a "metate" to grind "cocoa" to make chocolate candies and cocoa.

Arabesque Interior in "La Casa de Don Juan de Vargas," Tunja

Also of note: the stairway with the Spanish Arabesque wooden grillwork, in Mudéjar style, small columns worm eaten by now and a "vargueño" or fold up chair-desk from Spain. It was an extraordinary museum.

THE CHURCH OF SANTA CLARA

Ay ay ay. More Churches. Now the Church of Santa Clara.

Gold Altar of the Church of Santo Domingo, Tunja

It was highly ornamental, similar to the photos we saw of the original Santo Domingo (above) with the altars ("tablados") of red planks and gold adornment, and with the "altar mayor" in gold leaf with many paintings on its sides. The church dates from 1578 and is the first convent of the Clarisas from France and Rome. There was only one nave, very Baroque in style. To the side of the convent we saw the cell of Sister ("Sor") Josefina de Castillo, a nun-mystic-poetess born in Tunja in 1571 (she was the supposed relative-ancestor of a friend from Rockhurst days, Rafael Garófalo of Bogotá). She wrote "mystical" literature and is known as "Santa Jesus Colombiana." We saw her cell with the tiny, leather covered bed (hard as a rock), a tiny table and the chair where she wrote, and her "herramientas," steel tools for penitence ("silicio y flagelación"). Shades of today's Opus Dei as depicted in the movies! There is an even tinier cell off and above this one to where she would retreat for a greater period of meditation and silence. The walls were whitewashed but stained, supposedly with the blood of her flagellation! "A pity," said the nun who showed us her cell." ("Una pena según la monja que nos mostró la celda.") This then is the famous "Madre Castillo." Some writers like to compare her to the better known mystics of Spain—Santa Teresa de Jesus of Ávila and San Juan de la Cruz.

THE CHURCH OF SANTA BÁRBARA

It seemed similar to Santo Domingo, in the Baroque style and dating from 1599, with ceilings similar to Santa Clara, paintings of angels in the style of Zubarán and its high altar of gold leaf. There was a very interesting side altar with the Niño Jesus dressed in contemporary clothes! Shirt and slacks. "Gotta be a mistake,!" I wrote in my notes. Supposedly the ornamental clothing of the images was made for the saints by Juana la Loca, wife of King Felipe el Hermoso de España! I guess it was all the stitching.

We polished off the day with a visit to Bolívar Park with its famous "paredón;" behind glass are the bullet holes where several of the heroes prior to Independence were shot by the Spaniards!

This indeed was a record day of tourism on the trip. I wanted to see the Spanish Colonial Heritage of Colombia and we got it up to our ears. Exhausting. After being told we would not be able to "see anything," we wondered what we missed. Ha.

Church of the Jesuits, Tunja

On the last day in Tunja we arrived at a Jesuit church or at least in name, the "Iglesia de San Ignacio," totally restored, beautiful and different. There were plain, brick walls with many arches with a beautiful play of light through them, and a beautiful gold leaf altar. The grace of the place was its simple beauty, a welcome change from the Baroque excess described earlier. And the best was the piped in classical music reverberating in the church.

LA CASA DE CAPITÁN GONZALO SUÁREZ RENDÓN

Patio, "Casa del Capitán Rendón," Tunja

Interior Ceiling Paintings, "Casa del Capitán Rendón," Tunja

The local tourist guide (in Rotarian tone) says this is a "unique" house in all of Latin America—the "Mudéjar" influence in the "alfices" that crown the arches. The ceiling is painted like the Casa de Don Juan de Vargas and La Casa de Don Juan de Castellanos. The paintings were previously covered and hidden for a time. Themes are "Americanist,"—fauna and flora—with the family coats of arms in the style probably taken from that of Mateo Mirián el Viejo of 1616. The paintings however were done well after the original construction. There were fragments of shields on the walls that were the basis for the big shield on the main plaza of Tunja that says "Vencedor, Nunca Vencido," "Conqueror, never conquered." There were many tapestries and the coats of arms of Rendón, his wife's family, his sons, all gifts from Spain.

So ended the rather intense look at the Spanish Colonial heritage in Tunja, Boyacá.

THE PANTANO DE VARGAS

Monument of the "Pantano de Vargas"

Closer View, Monument of the "Pantano de Vargas"

What followed was a trip to the "Vargas Swamp" "Pantano de Vargas." The visit was a hoot! The Pantano de Vargas is in a big valley which was previously a swamp, hence the name. Once again it involves a military campaign in the battle for Independence, but this one was complicated. Bolívar's army came from the north and had to cross the swamp and Río Chicamoch by balsa raft. The Spaniards came from the south, discovered Bolivar's troops and surprised them, taking an early advantage. When all appeared lost, General Suárez Rendón came to the rescue with a famous charge with 14 lancers and thus swinging things to Bolívar's advantage. He of course wins the battle and Spanish General Barreiro flees to Paipa.

All this will later set the scene for the final decisive battle being The Battle of Boyacá. But the Pantano battle was according to our guide "the most decisive of the battles of the War of Independence." The peon guide had the entire story memorized including very dramatic and verbatim quotations from God knows where or whom. As I translated for Keah, he then repeated the last words, recorder-like, and continued while scratching his vitals, looking around in an exceedingly boring way. Keah and I were restraining ourselves to not laugh openly. The monument by the way is very striking: a concrete structure with 15 soldiers on horseback, 7 on either side and Rondón at their head. Colombians take all this very seriously; it was indeed a major battle for the northern campaign and would make Bolívar famous.

LA HOSTERÍA UCUENGUÁ

Keah and the Hostería Ucuenguá, Boyacá State

Mark. The Patio of the Hostería Ucuenguá

We had taken the bus from Tunja, asking the driver to let us off at Ucuenguá, and walked up the long lane to the "Hostería." The "Hostería" is on an old farm ("finca") of the Alarcón family and has some 20,000 rose bushes ("matas de rosales"). In each room there is a flower vase with a dozen roses with more in the bath. The towel comes wrapped in a red ribbon and with packets of toiletries (including Alka Seltzer!). The furniture is all in colonial style, many pieces covered in woolen mantels, and there are many leather trunks, wooden and leather chairs, a closet in "Mudéjar" style and huge wooden beams in the ceiling. Crystal lamps are in each room and each has wooden balconies and beautiful fountain outside. Up to this point this is tops for Colombian residences and hotels! Yet it really is a country inn, albeit, famous.

We were alone at breakfast in the restaurant of la "Hostería;" it consisted in fruit salad, chocolate, coffee, and cheese sandwiches. Plates are of copper with silver service. Outside the windows one sees only flowers and gardens. There were pretty candelabras and dark furniture of wood and leather. I wrote, "This is the finest place we have experienced in hotels in our travels!" I might add, up to that point!

EL MUSEO DE ARTE RELIGIOSA EN DUITAMA

We flagged down the "buseta" that comes past every fifteen minutes and went to the "Museo de Arte Religiosa" in Duitama. It was unique, as the tourist guides say, "the best of its kind" in the entire country. It sits on an old hacienda, once was a vacation house of the Jesuits and is now a museum. There were several large display rooms, three big patios, wooden columns and tiled roof. We saw paintings, images of saints, some of the latter very impressive including a Madonna about six feet tall in gold leaf and realist in style—from Spain. There was a "terrific" in the sense of terror, Christ figure which showed the seven wounds, a bloody back, skin cut to the ribs and spinal cord, the image full of blood. The style was once again the "Quiteño" of the 16th century.

Most impressive was a steel vault with chalices, gold monstrances ("custodias de oro"), emeralds, precious stones, wine cruets ("vineros"), and the gold boxes to take the sacred host to the sick ("cajetas para llevar la hostia al enfermo,)" all in a richness and art that was ostentatious, but beautiful. Such displays of the colonial church came to symbolize class differences and the later violent Liberal rebellion against the rich and the church hierarchy in many places in Latin America, especially Mexico in the 19th and 20th centuries. No wonder the churches are locked up tight and in many cases emptied of their treasures. Bank vaults do a good business.

Worthy of mention was the bus ride back to Dutama. This bus was the worst we had ever seen in Colombia—broken springs, lurching lopsided down the road, no windows, open motor visible from the inside of the bus, in sum, a disaster. After limping into town we went to woolen shops, "ruana' shops, etc., and we bought our tickets for the local firemen's benefit—an amateur bullfight with steers, a Mexican, a Venezuelan and an acrobat as toreros.

In Duitama there was a fine "almuerzo" of "pollo al horno," carrots, beets, cabbage, onions, french fries, beans and rice. After that we needed a quiet walk in the plaza and it was a pleasant experience, relaxing once again—talk with young girls headed to high school, lively, curious about English and charming they were! All were in the school uniforms: blue sweaters, plaid skirts, and white socks. "Well raised" ("Bien educadas") I thought.

Then we did a short side trip by bus some eleven kilometers from Duitama to Nobsa. As one goes north, it becomes drier, and now the air was contaminated by a huge cement factory with ovens to prepare the lime and a little farther down the road, the steel foundry of Belencito (query: Bethlehem Steel?)

A note on the local transportation (recalling the "cucharacha" bus already described). It is cheap, efficient and plentiful for the poor here, but is old and dirty. I wondered what the local gentry were thinking of the Americans who stay in luxury inns yet ride filthy buses instead of taking taxis?

We then repaired to more comfortable surroundings, the bar at the Ucuenguá: once again replete with colonial furniture, wooden and leather, carpet of woven straw of the region, a huge fireplace, bronze and silver stirrups decorating the walls, light in the form of artificial candles, classical music on a good sound system and fine "anís" or "aguardiente" of Colombia, that of the licorice flavor. This is where we caught up on these travel notes, a nice way to do it.

AN OUTING TO SOGAMOSO AND MONGUÍ

Alas, Mark is suffering greatly from stomach disorder plus a bad back. Maybe it's the fine food.

From the Hostería de Ucueguá we did a short side trip to Punta Larga, a colonial furniture factory, resort and chapel. It is the "Ethan Allen's" of Colombia with beautiful Spanish colonial furniture—rockers, wooden chests, beds and night tables ("varguenos, camas y mesaderas"). It has a pretty colonial style chapel and for 350 pesos, 11$ U.S., one can get a beautiful room; for 500 pesos you can get an entire floor of a house. There are green gardens which are sumptuous and beautiful and the price includes talking parrots. There is also an "artesanía" or folk art shop across the street.

The next morning after breakfast at the Ucuenguá, then the slow local into Duitama, a nice ride because it goes so slowly and you can see the cattle and sheep ranches, we caught a "rápido" to Sogamoso. There were many small "fincas" along the way, cattle, sheep, and you pass by the Hacienda Suescún. The visit in Sogamoso was very short and it did not impress us much. The main church was interesting for the stained glass windows, one large one behind the central nave, of Christ, mosaic on the side altars, obviously very different from most of the colonial churches we have seen. The small plaza was green and pretty.

Then we took a "buseta" from Sogamoso to Monguí. You go by the huge steel mill called "Paz del Río" with a lot of smoke, contamination and visible poverty nearby. Then the bus began a gradual climb passing farms with onions, carrots and wheat. Monguí is a very old town, a point of departure for the "missions" heading out to the "llanos" in Southern Colombia which eventually lead to the Amazon in the South. The town dates to the 16th century and is situated on the side of a mountain whose slope falls to the river.

Plaza de Monguió as Viewed from the Church

The entire town was cobblestoned and there was a large plaza with flowers dominated by, what else, the church. The church itself was gigantic with coats of arms, shields and crosses sculpted in rock on the façade. Inside the main altar and lateral altars are of carved wood, with gold leaf. Most significant according to our guide is there are a total of 130 paintings by Gregorio Vásquez y Ceballos in this church alone. Legend has it that the painter got himself in trouble in Bogotá, something to do with his relationship with a nun. He had to flee the city and moved on to Monguió. In order to pay for his room and board with the Franciscans he painted and painted a lot. The oil paintings are impressive, but after a few, all seemed to blend together and one's lasting impression is of confusion. A final part of the story is that at some point someone wanted to sell the paintings to folks in England, the local parish priest recoiled from this idea and hid them all in a cave. This might explain how some seemed deteriorated. A better idea is that the church seemed very dark and dingy; centuries of candles and incense have done a number on it. The interior patio of its convent or cloister is pretty; this is the water color scene we purchased and have at home in Mesa. Then we caught a little "buseta" for the return trip to Sogamoso.

The "almuerzo" was a bit strange: pollo al horno (okay), cold "arepas", like a sort of cold pancake, and boiled potatoes with nothing on them. Stranger yet was that they offered no utensils; everyone digs in with their hands. For whatever reason, it was a disaster for my stomach. We then did a short "paseo" through town but ended up in the poor part with pigs in the streets. We tried to visit the local anthropological museum but Latino bureaucracy got the best of us. It was very hot and we were out in the sun; the patio of the museum was open and there were umbrellas and tables, but the guard would not let us go in and we were to simply rest until the museum opened. Tired, hot and out of sorts, we left. I do not believe we missed much; the lawn needed to be mowed and the windows of the museum were broken. We went to four or five banks in town trying to change money and had no luck even with travelers' checks in dollars. Sogamoso was not a highlight of Colombia for us. It was interesting in one small way. There were many burros with heavy packs of coal, driven by women and one understands supplying the town with fuel for heating.

LA HACIENDA SUESCÚN

Then things got better; we caught a "carro colectivo," like a Mexican "pesero," to the Hacienda Suescún a few miles outside of town. It is four hundred years old and originally belonged to a Venezuelan family. It later became a country place for the Jesuits (you may notice they did all right while they could). With their expulsion in 1767 from the country and all Spanish and Portuguese dominions, the place was obtained by the family Niño Reyes. It was a beautiful country estate, all immensely green with pastures and fields, lots of Holstein cattle, meadows, horses and flower gardens. You enter by a long country lane with huge eucalyptus trees lining the lane. The entire hacienda is walled.

Bell Tower of the Hacienda Suescún

To one side of the ranch house there is a real "Casa Grande" like in Brazil's northeast, and to the side of it a chapel with a small bell tower. The big house itself has several wings and is a one-story structure. Between each wing are gardens and patios covered with flowers, bougainvilleas, etc.

Behind the house are green pastures which gradually climb to a forest and small mountain. From up above (we took a walk there) you see the entire green valley.

Keah on the Varanda of the Hacienda Suescún

The house itself has a large "salon," or living room with fireplace and large chimney, game rooms, bar, dining room, guest rooms and patios. There are many open "corredores" and "varandas" with flowers everywhere. After an afternoon walk around the place, when we returned the lady-owner showed us her private quarters. There is a register with messages from the famous guests— Colombian presidents except Rojas Pinilla the dictator. She claims all the presidents of Colombia have lodged there, including . . . Simón Bolívar . . . who stayed in room number 1. I believe her. She lives in Bogotá during the week and comes to the ranch on weekends. It was rather cool outside; we then retired, as it were, to the huge bar area in front of a comfortable fire and hearth and did our writing and had our drinks.

Dinner that evening was a memorable formal dining area occasion: juice, soup with sherry, meatballs, roast beef, mashed potatoes, dessert and coffee (jugo de tomate, sopa de jeréz, tarrarines con carne molida, rosbif, puré de papas, postre y café). We were served, alone in the dining room, by two waiters in white livery including gloves and a resplendent maitre'd who managed all manner of hot plates to keep the food the correct temperature, very formal. Keah always remembers this meal, and so do I in spite of being uncomfortable in those circumstances ("you can take the boy out of the country . . .) I think I could handle it better now, many years later.

Mark on the Lane of the Hacienda Suescún

Next day. We had breakfast out on the varanda of the big house, me thinking that more than one president of Colombia had probably done the same and sat perhaps at the same table. We took another walk around the farm, this time with the black Lab "Teo," taking many photos in the cool and incredibly fresh and sweet smelling air. One recalls our elegant departure: we walked down the long, eucalyptus lane with belongings in hand and waited at the end of the lane for our "rápido" to take us back to Duitama. You had to raise your hand to hail them. We wanted to encounter the "directos," but they did not seem to want to stop for some foreigners. At any rate, we decided to walk toward town (Sogamoso the nearest) and perhaps get a ride on the way. Imagine the scene; green fields full of cattle, sheep, and peasants planting corn and beans, all while we lugged our bags toward the nearby town.

LA LAGUNA DE TOTA

After one half-hour we caught a local back to our "favorite" hangout—Sogamoso. From there we caught what was a very tranquil bus heading up to "La Laguna de Tota." There was beautiful green countryside as we gradually climbed to the high "páramo" or plain, where they plant barley, wheat and onions. The local houses were of sticks, mud, and thatch. Peasants wear black "ruanas" and felt hats. We saw them doing the old fashioned thrashing of wheat from the straw. It seemed to be a highly populated area with a lot of cultivation. Finally, from a view from high above, the entire lake was covered with fog. I would estimate the lake was 6 by 16 kilometers large with many small, cultivated islands. There is a good paved road along one side that leads to the town of Aquitania. The water was clear but quite low due they say to a very dry year. There is a pretty local hotel called "Hotel Rocas Lindas." We were interested in the local fishing, supposedly for trout which they say go up to eight pounds! But there was no provision for rental of rods, reels, equipment of any kinds ("cañas o carreles"). And there is only good fishing, "buen pique," from 5-9 in the morning and 5-8 in the evening. So we ended up in the middle of the day hanging around the hotel, enjoying the sunshine and remembering better fishing days in Colorado.

After about an hour, we flagged down a bus to take us back down, a local full of "campesinos," but with piped in music—country songs from the U.S. including Marty Robbins, incredible when you think about it. The music blares on almost all the buses for "ambiente" or atmosphere, generally "bamberos" or Colombian country rhythms. It reminded me of the "Música Pindín" of friend Val de la Guardia (related to past presidents of Panamá) from Saint Louis University days. Val, in an aside, with his quite wealthy buddies, rich Cuban exiles, formed a little Latino band playing in Rogers hall, the girls' dorm, back in the mid—1960s. (I think mainly to connect with the coeds.) The campesinos on our bus had huge bags of onions, so we had a scent-filled ride back down the mountain. The ride was interesting with the Indian peasants, the local types that got on, along with the music back to Sogamoso.

The bus was called the "Gacela de Duitama," "The Gazelle of Duitama," not a misnomer, for there was an incredibly fast and stupid run back to Duitama. Arriving in town we had lunch and bought tickets for the big event tomorrow—a bull fight—from a pickup truck with loud speakers blaring advertising in the plazas. There are posters all over town, a big, big event. A sudden stomach-like sickness hit Keah in town and I had to be in emergency mode to find her a "baño" in a private residence. This is a perennial problem of public facilities in Latin America, a matter not to be taken lightly. And they charged for the service.

Lady Luck determined we would once again meet the ugly bus driver with his even uglier bus, the old "cucaracha," by now a love-hate relationship to us, to take us home to the Ucenguá Inn once more. I can safely say it is the worst public transportation I have encountered in twenty years of travel in Latin America, bar none. It was a grey, lopsided disaster headed down the road, belching smoke, loud noise and with the fearsome driver out of THE GOOD, THE BAD AND THE UGLY faithfully behind the wheel. I hope he gets an award plus a pension for keeping that thing going. One time when it did not start, he pulled a hose out of somewhere and primed the motor with gas, then he stopped for gas at a gas station and we finally proceeded. It was a case of "All aboard," and for those familiar with the vicissitudes of the carrier, passengers who joked and carried on the entire time. A good show it was.

We had a bit of a misunderstanding ("mal-entendido") about our room—a lack of hot water. Upset, but all settled in with new flowers in the room, we did a short walk along the Río Chochigota, the rose gardens, and the path by the river with burros pastured nearby. We returned to hot water, showers, and drinks in the bar-hogar of the Hostería.

A Two Fisted Drinker, the Indian Lady in the Market of Duitama

The next day began with breakfast of fruit, chocolate and cheese sandwiches and then the "Cucaracha" to town. We first visited the Duitama market. There was one large section with foodstuffs—fruits, cereals, vegetables, chickens, beef, bread and fish; then there was another with tools and household gadgets, another of clothing including "ruanas," felt hats, and finally another of straw objects, and baskets of all shapes. Apparently a lot of people come in from the country for the market. The women wear a large "panelón negro," that is, a black shawl with fringe, straw hats with a ribbon around them, and huge skirts. Most of them were drinking warm beer "al clima." Note the photo of an old, toothless woman drinking two at the same time while she was selling her articles. There were very few tourists or foreigners on this trip north, but there indeed has been lots of "local color."

We attended mass in Duitama; most people were dressed quite somberly in dark colors; there were many poor people, the men in dark clothing with dark "ruana" and women in black. The church was poor even by Colombia standards.

THE COUNTRY BULL FIGHT IN DUITAMA

Country Bull Fight, Duitama

It is a difficult task to describe it all; suffice to say it was one of the most picturesque moments I have experienced in Latin America over the years. It was a charity affair organized by the firemen of the town or region of Duitama, evidently the tenth anniversary of the event. Thus one explains all the commotion, and the blaring speakers of the p.a. system mounted on the pickup-fire truck announcing the event. There was not properly speaking a "plaza de toros" here permanently. There was, however, a vacant field around which they had constructed an arena and shaky bleachers entirely out of wood, all in a completed oval. It seemed hastily constructed and not too stable. When we arrived there were all kinds of people sitting on the grass outside the arena, singing, drinking wine from the "bota" I described earlier in Medellín—a real cow's hoof and lower leg hollowed out to make the "bota" or flask. And I saw a few of the "legitimate" leather "botas" of goat skin one associated with Spain.

The firemen were all there with their old fashioned red helmets and the policemen with their night sticks. All seemed highly unorganized. The "producer" or "empresario" of the "corrida" was an old man who had not shaved for several days and was indeed grizzly, wearing very poor clothing and a "ruana." But it was clear he was in charge of the livestock. Another colorful type was the rancher who had brought the stock, a "llanero." He was very colorful and played his role to the hilt: the traditional flat brimmed felt "gentleman's" hat from Spain, an old worn suit but in addition, he sported a leather whip he brandished throughout the day. He also had a bottle of "aguardiente" he kept in his hip pocket and offered freely to friends, then taking a swig himself.

People now began to enter the stands, some already fairly drunk from their "botas." We purchased a bottle of "manzanilla" or apple wine just to ward off the chill. I feared that the bottles would later be thrown into the ring, but people evidently did not have that custom. Most of the people did not come into the stands until the "toreros" arrived aboard another fire engine. There was a band stationed high up in the bleachers on the opposite side to us and it played more dance music than bullfight music.

Surprisingly enough, three of the four bulls were good, and one of the "toreros" was impressive as well, making passes on his knees with his back to the bull, "verónicas" I think they are called, but he fell down twice. The bulls were "Zebu" or Brahma stock from the "llanos." The bull fighters killed three bulls but without the use of the "picadores." They did use "banderillas" or short pointed sticks driven in by the bullfighters.

What was different and appeared to be the main attraction was a "torero" called "Superman" who was dressed like the comic book hero. The problem of course is that Superman is not easily imitated and this fellow was more like a caricature, a "caballero de la triste figura" type, like Quixote's imitation of a knight-errant. But the fellow did know how to fight the bull and killed his bull, being awarded two ears for his efforts. (I found myself thinking of the rodeo clown in the U.S. who is generally an extremely talented cowboy who decides to take on the much more dangerous task of bull-baiting.) This guy was also an "acrobatic bull fighter" ("torero acróbata.)" He brandished a sort of vaulting pole, would run toward the bull and easily vault over its charging horns. He also ran in front of the bull allowing his Superman cape (red of course) to attract and madden the bull as he teased, danced and feinted. At one point he sat on the bull's head and grabbed its tail and spun around a few times. But at the end he returned to the traditional style with "banderillas" first and then the "estoque" or sword.

Another clown type was also present, dressed like a woman, who would run into the arena for laughs. They let the last bull loose and people from the town could jump into the arena and take their chances. These were small Brahmas, not like the fighting bulls in Pamplona. By this time there were a lot of drunken folks, several of whom would jump the barrier and do their thing in the ring. An interesting aside: men would stand between the stands and the barrier, constantly watching the fight, and pee down the barrier wall. Was this a good way to not miss any action? At the end many people were dancing in the stands, and almost no one paid any attention to the action in the arena. It was rather a drunken brawl by the end. We escaped without any incidents and took the "Cucaracha" back home to the Ucenguá. This time there were many drunken Indians aboard, and the bus broke down as usual. I suspect this is the norm for the end of the Sunday market. So we walked the rest of the way back home for our last night in the Inn in the comfort of the bar with the fireplace, writing a bit of our adventures before our departure the next day.

ON TO VILLA DE LEIVA

We hopped a bus to Punta Larga and then back to Tunja for connections to Villa de Leiva. There were more adventures at the tourist office in Tunja trying to change travelers' checks. This is the way it goes: a peon employee must type out a form, pass it along for signatures and approvals and then we wait in a long teller's line, generally an irritating process. This time a chain smoker tried to do it all and it was a trick to manage the smoking and the typing. It seems funny now, not then. There seemed to be a total lack of organization in the banks, like the line of authority. The overriding sensation was that this was the first time in their lives they had ever seen, much less cashed, a travelers' check.

Leiva is a bit off the beaten track, a special route and bus. We went down a lot in altitude and into dryer country. It looked like there were coal deposits in the hills, but it was a good paved road and the driver was sane. The bus left us on the side of the road outside of Leiva and we carried bags to the hotel. The town is small with some 8000 residents; it seemed about like Santa Fé de Antioquia. Villa de Leiva is a national monument and all the buildings are of colonial architecture, many the originals. The streets were all cobblestoned from the original time of 1572.

La Plaza, Villa de Leiva

The plaza was huge, one of the largest we have seen in the country; the Colombians claim it is the largest in the Americas! There is a small central fountain and the plaza is cobblestone, used as a parking lot, but now deserted. The aesthetic effect is one of austerity and simplicity; it seems pure, archaic and pretty.

Mark and the Columns of the Plaza of Villa de Leiva

There were few people in town the day we arrived; all was very tranquil. We walked around a bit, visited a few arts and crafts stores and then drank a beer at the side of the plaza. It was a beautiful time of day, that time just before sunset when the light is most punctuated with color; all seems very brilliant in the whiteness between the columns of the old buildings and the huge "portales" or doorways of the plaza.

OUR INN—EL MOLINO DE MESOPOTAMIA

Entrance to the Molino de Mesopotamia Inn

It is without doubt, and each day I seem to amend the entry of the day before, the best "parador, hotel, hostería" we have encountered in Colombia. It was constructed by a Spaniard in 1562 ten years before the Villa was founded. His descendants owned it until 1768 when it passed to the Neira family. The current hotel is twelve years old. The Inn is on the outskirts of town, and as per the name, it originally was and still is a flour mill. The basis for irrigation of its gardens is still from the spring from the hill in back of the Inn, large, pure and strong enough to turn the mill wheel for grinding grain into flour. There is in fact a large mill stone which today decorates the middle of the dining room. Canals from the spring flow into a pool above the Inn and irrigate and feed the various surrounding gardens.

Flowers and Patio, Molino de Mesopotamia Inn

El Molino de Mesopotamia and Mountain in the Background

This place is listed in the Colombian guidebooks as one of four or five outstandingly quaint places in all of Latin America. The hotel itself is behind a wall which is whitewashed with tiles on the top. Inside the wall one is surrounded by bougainvillea, roses, etc. There are diverse wings with rooms with gardens in between and brick walkways. Our room had a polished wooden floor, thick walls and a window looking out to long verandas with tile floors and wooden railings, surrounded by all manner of flowers. From the veranda you can see the patio full of flowers, the gardens, and over the low roof of the Inn you can see green pastures and the mountains beyond. The salon is full of antiques: sofas, lamps, straw floor coverings, and chairs and tables of carved wood. There is an old Victrola (the RCA original). In the rooms the beds are of carved wood and with canopies. And each room is full of ceramics from Ráquira (famous in the region.)

All meals were included with the tariff, and they were fine indeed. A note from that time and place is in order: the daily tariff with all meals for two people was 440 Colombian pesos, $16.00 dollars U.S. I noted the dinner that first evening in all its finery: pineapple juice, onion soup, filet mignon in a sauce, potatoes, dessert and coffee, all this in delightful surroundings. The reason I note it is that the next day I suffered from something I ate.

Or perhaps it was breakfast the following morning: pineapple juice, homemade bread cooked in the Inn, fried eggs, cheese, and hot chocolate. It is all European plan, so meals are included in the tariff.

Two black Scotty dogs are the mascots of this place.

THE COLONIAL HERITAGE IN VILLA DE LEIVA

Colonial Street Scene, Villa de Leiva

Convent of the "Carmelitas Descalzas," Villa de Leiva

We walked easily to the downtown and visited the Iglesia del Carmen. There is still a cloistered nuns' community here with eighteen nuns of the "Carmelitas Descalzas," the order founded by Santa Teresa de Jesus in Ávila,Spain. The church was pretty, but simple in style. This was our first visit to such a place; it seemed very Spanish and very medieval.

HISTORY IN VILLA DE LEIVA

Coat of Arms, the Royal Liquor Distillery, Villa de Leiva

We visited the Home of the First Congress of the United Provinces of Colombia ("Casa del Primer Congreso de las Provincias Unidas de Colombia") from 1812. This is where the "Acta de Independencia" was written and signed by Camilo Torres of "Memorial de Agravios" fame and was also the house where Antonio Nariño died (he was the translator of "The Rights of Man" ("Los Derechos del Hombre"), important for the entire era of Independence. One could say it is Colombia's Philadelphia, sort of. After translating this famous work by the French philosopher Rousseau, Nariño was incarcerated in Spain, returned to Colombia in 1821 and was killed in 1823.

A needed respite: that p.m. we went shopping for ceramics and Indian belts in Villa de Leiva, had a beer in the plaza, mass in the plaza church, but enjoyed music by a "Tuna" afterwards (the musical group associated with Santiago de Compostela in Spain; it is comprised of students in medieval dress with many tunes, ribald humor and a penchant for having fun). That evening at the

Mespotamia we had a dinner of salmon, and Mark was sick again. So sick that I ate no breakfast the following morning.

MOVIE MAKING IN COLOMBIA

Making Movies in Colombia, the Blond German Hero and the Black Colombian "Nuns"

We were surprised to encounter a full blown production now going on in the huge main plaza. It was curious to see, a product of the times. The production was a German-Italian B Western (Spaghetti Westerns were the current rage) with a sprinkling of Colombians in the cast. It was just like in the movie magazines, but funnier. The players were the hero, a tall, blond, Aryan German type, a short, dark "bobo" or "gracioso" (the clown for comic relief) played by an Italian, Colombian heroines—black actresses who were beautiful and dressed as nuns, and a German director, Assistant Director from Italy, with German cameras and operators. There were huge white lights and cameras.

We saw several takes from scenes, one in which the hero jumps down to the street from a second floor window and then runs off. Another when the "bobo" hangs suspended from a thick hangman's noose and is to be cut down and fall onto a burro beneath, backwards that is, on the burro. They did three takes. The first time he fell but not onto the burro; the second was ruined when a local kid ran through the scene with the camera running. They got it the third time. The title of the movie was: "Dos Vagabundos," "Two Vagabonds."

There was another scene which they redid several times (perhaps at the request of the German director): the "bobo" had to run all the way across "the largest plaza in the Americas" while yelling something. There were several takes, so we felt sorry for the ole' boy.

Not ones to miss a meal at the Mesopotamia, we returned for lunch: stew, fruit salad, rice etc. It was raining cats and dogs so we stayed in until 4 p.m. After the rain the "paseo" through the town with that pure, clean air was delightful, and there was a pleasantly cool temperature. We walked to the outskirts of the town, checking out the Hotel-Convento San Francisco and the Hospedería Nariño, then the parroquial church, poor, dark and robbed of its treasures.

Maybe it was the supper that did it: more juice, cream of tomato soup, puré de papas, and a soufflé of "coajuada," German Sausage that is, flan and coffee. All sickness in honor of the German actor.

Thinking about Villa de Leiva, there is an atmosphere which is uncluttered or spoiled; one can see why it is a natural for movies. Many peasants ride through town on mules, burros or on foot. We could be living in the 16th century.

THE "ECCE HOMO" MONASTERY

On the next day after a breakfast of "huevos pericos con tocineta," orange juice, chocolate, etc. we took off on a small adventure with three young Colombians, Gustavo, Eduardo (Flaco) and Alfonso in their car. Did you ever have an intuition or vibes that all would not turn out well? They were all very "vivos," intelligent and entertaining and were the most organized Colombian tourists I have ever seen with maps and a time table for everything, totally un-Latino. They made a record of everything with photos, notes on milage, etc.

The group left Villa de Leiva in the morning, stopped first at El Cárcamo, an old mill now a hacienda. Juan José Neira, one of the precursors of Independence lived here. They raise chickens so we looked at them for a while and saw some dove hunters with shotguns.

We then arrived at a highlight of that area of Colombia, the Ecce Homo Monastery.

The Monastery of Ecce Homo

111

The Patio of the Monastery of Ecce Homo

This is one of three famous stone edifices in all Colombia (the others are San Felipe Fortress in Cartagena and El Salitre in Paipa).The monastery dates from 1620 when it was founded by Dominican priests as a training center for the Spanish Catholic missions headed out to the "llanos." Some say its architecture and style are patterned after that of the Escorial in Spain and they add that it is the most "Spanish" cloister in all Colombia. Today it is a retreat house. A very happy, smiling nun explained it all to us, adding a little "holy" myth which reminded me of friend Eduardo Matheu's mother Concha and her tales in Guatemala. The latter had many stories of old times in Guatemala, of the nuns, the legends, and all in a sing-song, storybook voice for children. This nun at Ecce Homo told a story that went like this: "Once upon a time there was a lady who owned all the land nearby, and she was a penitent, making her own crown of thorns and wearing it about (she said almost happily). St. Bartholomew appeared to her in a vision and commanded that she build a convent on the spot."

Anyway . . . after its mission days Ecce Homo became the local parish church. Spanish General Santander prior to independence days took it over to use as a barracks for his army. After Independence, Bolívar returned it to the priests to serve as a monastery. The inside of the church did not seem much different from what we had been seeing in Colombia (or was this tourism waning in us), but the convent is impressive for the columns and the patio, all in stone construction.

ARRIVAL IN RÁQUIRA

The jaunt continued, now to a place called Ráquira known for its ceramics. We had a flat tire in a little town called Sutamarchá, and the spare tire was flat. After taking two nails out with my small fishing knife, we did the temporary fix with one of those bottles of compressed goo. I expected the boys to fix the flat, but they continued on with the temporary job on the rim. I can attribute our safe trip only to the fact it was St. Joseph's day in Colombia.

The Church of Ráquira and Its Ceramics

We arrived in Ráquira with its small, quaint plaza which is surrounded by large works of ceramic placed on an ironwork fence surrounding the plaza as well as on the pedestals of the entrance of the church. Many of the objects were or looked like mythical animals, and some also depicted Indian figures. For a town in the middle of nowhere it all seemed quite extensive to us, but the locals seemed in no hurry to sell anything. I did note that many people were drinking beer "al clima" and there were a few drunks. Does making ceramics all day drive one to drink?

After Ráquira we did make it safely back to Villa de Leiva, picking up two kids who had been fossil hunting in the area, famous for the same. After lunch in the Villa we all piled into the Fiat and with the three Colombian students made a very rapid return to Bogotá. On the way we saw green "sabanas," the mini-fundia of Boyacá, and oxen plowing along with their peasant owners in the fields. We passed the Puente de Boyacá again and made a fast run to Zipa. Keah and I missed the bus there, so the good hosts ran us on into Bogotá in a frightening ride. We arrived just in time for the frantic, it seemed, preparation for Carol (Emery) and Alvaro's flight back to the U.S. a trip to Los Angeles where Álvaro would attend an intensive English course.

FINAL BUSINESS IN BOGOTÁ

I've not said too much about shopping in Colombia, but we did a good amount of it, hunting mainly for handicrafts and folk art. Many of these items still decorate our house in Mesa, Arizona. This last day in downtown Bogotá we went with Jim for shopping, a silver necklace for Keah, one more "ruana," and for Mark some books and the tourist slides promised by the Colombian tourist commission. If one announced one's association with an American university and a sincere effort to "publicize" Colombia, good things happened. Then we had our only experience with Colombia's famous emeralds. Jim took us to the high scale store of Bronkeys and we learned a bit about emeralds: color, size, purity, looking for "inclusions or "fuego." They were indeed beautiful, but small in size compared to the Brazilian semi-precious stones of my time in Brazil in the 1960s, but of much greater value.

There was a brief session talking to Aerolineas Colombianas about a possible summer school in Colombia by ASU. I cannot remember details, but nothing came of it in the end.

TRIP TO ZIPAQUIRÁ

This would be our final local outing from Bogotá. We climbed into yet another Colombian bus for the last trip in the highlands, first passing through the north zone of Bogotá, traveling in my opinion on a very dangerous freeway. Drivers seemed to use it to test the uttermost speed and capabilities of their vehicles (I thought of ASU Italian Professor Pier Baldini telling of freeway roads in the Pyrenees of north Italy where there is no speed limit other than your own fears). Once off the freeway and onto the two lane roads things slowed down and we could appreciate the green countryside and large dairy farms with Holstein stock. We learned it is a custom to get out of town on Sunday in Bogotá for a Sunday ride and dinner in the countryside; that explains much. The buses were full of humble people heading for the country and Zipaquirá.

The main plaza of the town was crowded and festive. In front of all the buildings they were selling huge palm leaves some six feet tall. It was indeed Palm Sunday, so people buy them and take them into the church for the priest's blessing. There was much to do, making Palm Sunday in the U.S. seem insignificant.

The Salt Cathedral of Zipaquirá

Then we climbed the hill to Zipaquirá's main attraction—a former salt mine which now houses a cathedral within, carved from the pure salt sides. The entrance to the mine is wide and dark! The tunnels inside and the cathedral itself are huge, impressive for their size, the height of the ceilings, the columns inside, a huge wooden cross, the diffused light and a few images evidently carved from salt. It all seemed a bit eerie to me, somewhat dark, and a bit depressing. It was a sort of Catholic tourist trap.

Sure enough, outside we ran into the Otavalo Indians and their wares. I wondered, were these the same guys we saw in Silvia outside of Popayán? We bought more shawls, beautiful work in wool in fine colors, and in fact still use one placed below the Nativity Scene each Christmas. Then we attended mass with a full house. The return to Bogotá was in a comfortable bus, ah, with "música de ambiente." I did make a mental note comparing experience in Mexico City and Colombia: the buses in Mexico City in 1962 were frequented by strolling musicians who played for tips, but now we had the piped in "pasa-cintas," or tape decks of the 1970s.

RETURN TO BOGOTÁ: LAST EVENING WITH THE EMERYS

I can describe the family well since we got to know them and their routines well. This was a very communicative, good Christian family. We, the Roman Catholics, were well treated and are better people for the experience which was truly ecumenical and healing I believe, perhaps on both parts. This was the first time I had ever really shared with Protestant, Missionary types who seemed totally rational and with high ideals. We left very thankful for the experience, much the wiser and feeling good about our friends. So thank you Jim for the whole idea and for incredible hospitality from your family.

PART IV. CARTAGENA DE INDIAS

CARTAGENA DE INDIAS—INTRODUCTION AND THE SPANISH TREASURE FLEET

The area was discovered by Rodrigo de Bastidas in 1501 and was officially founded in 1533 by Don Pedro de Heredia. The difference between one date and another was perhaps due to a lack of potable water in the city or to the presence of Carib Indians. But what stimulated interest in the site was the discovery of gold in Peru and Mexico and the establishment of the Spanish Flotilla System to effect commerce between Spain and the New World. The Spanish Fleet and its treasure ships, the Galleons, arrived from Spain to two major ports, Vera Cruz in Mexico and Cartagena in Colombia. The former would handle commerce from the Philippines and Mexico, the latter the riches from Peru. In the latter case, the fleet would sail from Spain with products for the fair on the Atlantic side of Panama but arrived first in Cartagena and there awaited news of the sailing of the Peruvian Fleet and its arrival on the Pacific Side of Panama. When the two joined in the Fair of Portobelo they sold products from Spain and loaded the rich metals from Peru for eventual shipping to Spain. Much of the actual business and negotiations took place in Cartagena where the fleet stayed for about four months prior to the arrival of the Pacific fleet in Panama. That is why the corsairs like Baal, el Draque, the Baron de Pointis, and Vernon attacked and sacked the city on several occasions. All had "unofficial" orders to "singe the beard of the Spanish King." Although Drake's attack was the most famous (he demanded and received ten million gold pesos to not burn the city after he sacked it in 1586; there is a receipt on record at the Casa de la Inquisicón in Cartagena. Honor amongst thieves!), the most ferocious battle was with the Englishman Vernon in 1741 (he demanded that they strike medals of the taking of Cartagena BEFORE he began his campaign).

All in all the Spanish kings during more than 300 years constructed an amazing series of fortifications to protect the city.

Cartagena also gained fame as the principal port for the entry of slaves into the Americas from the 16th through the mid—19th centuries. Commerce in the New World by the Spanish Crown was weakened by the discovery and rounding of Cape Horn and the Strait of Magellan, although trade through this route was officially illegal. But the effect was that the commerce between Panama and Cartagena gradually diminished. And it also lessened with the official granting of freedom to the slaves. Freedom of commerce was only officially recognized by Spain at the end of the 18th century under the Borbon dynasty, and that rejuvenated Cartagena to some degree. Today the city is known for tourism and maritime commerce.

THE DEFENSE OF CARTAGENA

Due to its richness corsairs and pirates attacked and sacked the city on various occasions, the most important being that of Sir Francis Drake in 1586. Therefore the Spanish kings during more than 300 years constructed an amazing series of forts to protect the city as well as constructing a wall around the old city. It is or was a "city fortress." The old city walls around Gethsimane Plaza are four meters high and five meters thick, but in spite of this the city was sacked several times. The Spaniards spent, according to one statistic, more than 69 million ounces of gold in the fortification of the city, the largest defensive network in the New World and perhaps in the old.

The Spaniards did not fear an attack from the north due to the reef, but still placed batteries within the walled old city, batteries named with saints' names like St. Ignatius of Loyola or St. Francis Xavier, to resist the impact of cannons and other fire arms. The batteries of the old city are united by this "curtain of walls," a total of 23 batteries by the 18th century. In spite of this in 1586 Sir Francis Drake ("el Draque") assaulted and took the city. As a result King Felipe II of Spain commanded that a larger defense effort be made, another fearful series of forts and batteries. As mentioned, an attack from the north (the Caribbean Ocean) was impossible due to the reefs. Therefore the invaders entered via Boca Grande up to the middle of the 18th century when the wrecks of ships closed the entrance. Then an exceptionally high tide caused a sand bar to be formed and closed that entrance for more than one hundred years.

So the defense of the Plaza then centered upon Boca Chica to the west (this was the epoch of Vernon in 1741). A series of forts were constructed, most to be mentioned later in the narrative. But the granddaddy of them all would be San Felipe de Barajas. Interestingly enough, later Boca Grande opened up again due to a change in ocean currents after Vernon's attack. So the Spaniards then constructed an underwater reef in 1771, closing Boca Grande indefinitely. After all this, due to curious and ironic luck, the Spaniards themselves had to confront this same line of defense in 1810 when the patriots took control of Cartagena. The Spanish general, Don Pablo Morillo, in 1815 was left with the decision to set siege to the city to reduce it to hunger and thus defeat. He succeeded through this tactic, thus never having to take military action against the forts which thus remain intact today as a monument to military architecture in the colony.

SEARCHING FOR THE COLONIAL HERITAGE

Our extensive time in Cartagena was to see and study the history of the place and to witness perhaps the greatest example of Spanish military architecture in America.

Our stay in Cartagena began with the flight on the big Aero Condor jet from Bogotá to Cartagena. I noted that on one of the flights leaving the Bogotá airport, a four engine prop, a man stood by with a fire extinguisher as the propellers began to turn. Unsettling. Anyway, on its landing in Cartagena I was able to take photos of Boca Grande from the air. The airport has a big mountain to one side, the sea to the other, making for beautiful and dangerous landings. From the old city and the district of Gethismane with its walls there is an avenue which takes you by way of the ocean and out to the hotel district in Boca Grande. It was a beautiful drive, less than a dollar by taxi in 1975.

Boca Grande is beautiful with the luxury hotel district facing the sea, nice homes, restaurants and shops. There is an atmosphere of sea, beach and tourism. We stayed at the Hotel Americano, old, a bit worse for wear, not too well cared for, but the right price and still in Boca Grande. And it is on the beach; the sand is brown, not at all as pretty as the beaches in the Northeast of Brazil. The area did remind me a bit of Barra Avenida in Salvador, Bahia, Brazil. However the water close to the beach is dirty; at least it was when we were there; one has to go far out before it is green-blue. But it was not deep either, so you can wade far out and the waves are smaller, but there is an "empuje" or undertow. There were both dark and white people on the beach and what seemed a mixture of rich and poor. Blacks are in the majority here; you see black ladies with huge baskets on their heads selling fresh slices of pineapple. Shades of Carmen Miranda! There were lots of young kids, mainly teenagers on vacation (Holy Week in Cartagena). We immediately put on suits and went for a walk on the beach and a swim.

The culinary discovery in Cartagena (on Jim Emery's advice) was Mee Wah's where we had "langostino agrio y dulce." It was one of the best discoveries made in Colombia; there was oriental music in the background, a huge tapestry with an image of a tiger, and good food.

Our visit would combine tourism with a more serious look at the major historic sites in the city, and the narration weaves the two together.

FIRST FORAY INTO THE OLD CITY

LA TORRE DEL RELOJ

The "Torre del Reloj" Watch Tower of Cartagena

We took a taxi from the Boca Grande district and got out in front of the "Watch Tower" ("Torre del Reloj") opposite the docks where there were many cargo boats docked, many with sails. It was very, very busy. We walked through the arches into the section of the old city called Gethsimane, the old city being completely surrounded by walls. After Sir Francis Drake sacked the city in 1586 King Felipe II commanded the wall to be built and also the construction of more fortresses. The walls were impressive for their thickness and the cannons on top.

The "Portada" or Entrance of the House of the Inquisition, Cartagena

The Inside Patio of the House of the Inquisition

LA CASA DE LA INQUISICIÓN

From the "Torre del Reloj" we walked to the main plaza in the old city; you might have guessed the name, "Plaza Bolívar." The next stop was the "Casa de la Inquisición." The original edifice was seriously wrecked by Admiral Vernon's attack in 1740 and the current one was built at that time. The huge doorway "portal" is in the Baroque style of 1770 (the coat of arms of the original building had been destroyed). The Inquisition was established in Cartagena in 1610 with jurisdiction in all the Caribbean as far as Guatemala. Recall the age: the Inquisition served as a political arm since the government was Catholic and had a policy of searching out and punishing Jews, Heretics, sorcerers, witches and "relapsos" both fallen away Jews and Catholics. One might recall, for perspective, England's Tower of London and the deaths of Sir Thomas More and Mary Stuart. The Inquisition was respected in the beginning and hated and feared at the end. Note, however, that in all its existence in Cartagena only five people were put to death. Inside the building there are the quarters of the inquisitors, jail cells for heretics, etc. There are three floors: today on the first are government offices and tourism; on the second there is a small museum of colonial ways, on the third paintings and documents from the historical society of Cartagena.

There are old cannons in the patio, and there used to be on view all manner of articles for the torture of the prisoners (no longer). But you can still see the small windows of the prisoners' cells with bars on them. According to some sources (probably the office of tourism) this building is the best example of Spanish Colonial Architecture of the 18th century, just incidentally including thirty cells for prisoners and a torture room. They speak of two famous cases: an Englishman who refused to deny his faith and was burned at the stake, and a priest who was hung. The inquisitors were thrown out in 1811, returned in 1815 when the city was retaken by Spain in the name of the "Pacifier" ("Pacificador") Pablo Morillo, and thrown out again in 1821 when independence came to Colombia.

The Façade of the Church of San Pedro Claver

The Interior Patio of the Church of San Pedro Claver

THE CHURCH AND CONVENT OF SAN PEDRO CLAVER

Then we went to the church and convent of San Pedro Claver in the old city. The original convent is from 1603. The prettiest part is the interior garden surrounded by a three story convent with arches and columns. The church is said to be the "most important religious relic" in Colombia.

The present church is from the 18th century and did not exist during Peter Claver's time; then in 1770 it was known as San Juan de Dios, after the expulsion of the Jesuits. Today it is once again a Jesuit parish and the priests have their residence on the third floor. We were told they do social action projects for the poor neighborhoods of Cartagena. The church has little decoration, an altar of marble, and there are several stained glass windows with scenes from the life of San Pedro Claver. His body remains under the high altar in a glass casket. He was canonized in 1888. Today there is a museum on the first floor of the convent with oil paintings and a chapel in the room where he died. The total impression was of silence and grandeur with the old trees and the old rock stairs.

San Pedro Claver was born in Verdu, Catalonia, Spain, studied in Bogotá and Tunja, and was ordained in Cartagena. His life was dedicated to the care of slaves. He was supposed to have awaited the arrival of slave ships and boarded them to take care of the wounded and restoring the sick to health. Three hundred thousand slaves passed through Cartagena in his time. He catechized many of them as well. He died in 1654, "el apóstolo de los negros."

The San Ignacio Battery, the Walled Fort of Old Cartagena

After the visit to the Church of San Pedro Claver we walked along the sea wall facing the bay, looked at the cannons and the sea. The batteries are all named after Catholic saints. Then we walked along the docks; one can now take tour boats out to Boca Chica (the west, far end of the bay and its forts). We returned to Boca Grande and the hotel district, and once again enjoyed dinner at Mee Wah's—rice, shrimp, langostino chop suey with delicious vegetables.

THE OLD CITY OF CARTAGENA

Street Scene of Cartagena

There is a series of very narrow streets in the old part of the city and much now has been reconstructed.

The old houses have wooden balconies, shields or coats of arms, arches and patios. The streets were crowded; it reminded me a lot of the downtown of Recife, Brazil. (And I surmise it is much like the old parts of Puerto Rico, Cuba and other Caribbean countries. Forts like these can be seen in San Juan and even in St. Augustine in Florida.) The population was largely black and the climate was hot.

The Church of Santo Domingo and the "Crooked Tower"

THE CHURCH OF SANTO DOMINGO

It is the oldest in Cartagena, dating from 1550 and containing a miraculous image of the seated Christ with arms crossed. The convent of the said church is in the style of that of the church of San Pedro Claver of the 18th century. This church has what they call "estribos exteriores," "exterior stirrups," giving the name to the entire street, "Calle de los Estribos." The walls of the church are as thick as those of the walled defenses of the city of Caratagena. The irregularly shaped tower of the church has a legend explaining its "off-center" turn: "The devil did it!

THE CATHEDRAL OF CARTAGENA

It was begun in 1575 and was partially destroyed by "El Draque" in 1586. The central altar has three levels of images, all in gold gilt. The pulpit has many shades of marble. All the lateral altars are of marble, 17th century. As we visited they were practicing for Holy Week ceremonies. The church did not impress much on the inside other than its size, but the outside was impressive for its severe beauty.

Entrance Door, "Pórtico," La Casa del Marqués de Valdehoyos

Then we went to the famous Casa del Marqués de Valdehoyos. There is a large "portada" or entrance of sculpted stone and a huge exterior balcony on the second floor facing up and down the street. Inside there were several patios, nice fountains with refreshing water and the "caballeriza" or stable. The ground floor included the entrance from the street, stable and storage. Living quarters were on the "primer piso" or second floor in English terms. In the entryway there are stone pedestals to aid the mounting and dismounting of horses. The central patio is cloistered with wood arabesques. According to local legend, the Marqués slept in a different bedroom each night from fear of assassination. There are double balconies of wood. The large "salon" on the second floor faces the street and was a reception room with the ceiling in "Mozárabe" or "Mudéjar" style. The dining room is protected by "celosias" or wooden, arabesque screens. There is a spiral stairway up to the "mirador" or lookout where one can see most of the old city and the sea beyond. Back on the "planta baja" or ground floor there are deposits for grain, supplies, flour and the slave quarters. The Marqués had a monopoly on the latter during colonial days. He was originally from Oviedo in Spain, had four other houses in Cartagena and land in the Valle de Upar. He died in Havana in the 18th century but was succeeded by a son. The son committed so many atrocities on the Royalist side against the patriots in the war for independence that once defeated, he left for Peru where he was named mayor of La Paz (in Alto Peru). There he was assassinated by the natives for his despotic ways.

GOOD FRIDAY AND CHURCH SERVICES IN CARTAGENA

Holy Week Procession, Cartagena

We took the bus downtown where we went first to the cathedral, then to Santo Domingo and then to the sea wall. Of note was a Good Friday procession: images of Jesus carrying the cross and then the "Virgen Dolorosa" dressed in black. Many people were accompanying the procession as it formed a "Via Crucis" in the narrow streets of the old city. We then headed to the Plaza Bolívar in the old city; there is a local custom to make visits to all the major churches on Good Friday, so we complied. It was very hot, but it was interesting to sit in the shade of the plaza and see all the goings on. One understands why folks here take their time and walk slowly; the heat gets to you.

GOOD FRIDAY SERVICES

At San Pedro Claver there was a litany, sermon, communion and procession, but it was like a religious festival: everyone was talking in church like a family get-together. There were many buses with huge groups of tourists in the old city, and they would all enter together into the church. So it was not the somber, serious thing of Good Friday as in Catholic churches in the U.S.

At Santo Domingo before the procession everyone was waiting outside and the atmosphere was more like that of a parade than a religious ceremony. There was a band in white uniforms and a festive atmosphere. After the service in the church, they processed with the image of the Fallen Christ which in turn was followed by a band playing what I surmise was a funeral dirge. Then the "Dolorosa" that followed was carried by women, in spite of the size and weight of the statue. This procession winds through the city until it gets to San Pedro Claver. By now it is late afternoon and the church lights are on, a very pretty scene and unique atmosphere. Keah and I followed the procession like so many others of the general public (anyone is free to join). That probably was the most emotional part of the day, more so than being inside the church. I surmised this is the atmosphere in Sevilla, Spain, during Holy Week.

FORTIFICATIONS OF CARTAGENA

THE "CLUB DE PESCA" AND THE FORT OF SAN SEBASTIÁN DEL PASTELILLO

El Fuerte del Pastelillo

It is part of an old fort that faces the docks and old city walls and the Torre del Reloj. It was constructed in 1743 in place of the oldest fort of the city, "El Boquerón" of 16th century fame. It protected the "Bahía de las Ánimas" and was a lateral fort to the latter constructed San Felipe. The idea was to provide crossfire against vessels attacking the old city from the bay. It is of irregular design, shaped a bit like a cake, thus the name "pastel." The restaurant of today sits where the barracks used to be. The fort is built at sea level so its guns could be aimed directly at enemy vessels at water level. It is basically a large "paralelepipedo" or rectangle with "almenas, torneras, garitas esquineras, y aspelleras para fusilerría." It also served as a port, dock, ammo depot and barracks.

From the Club (I recall the nice photo through the porthole window of the men's room) one could see in 1975 beautiful yachts, sail ships from the U.SA. and other places. From this luncheon spot one could also see a navy depot in the harbor and the outline of the old city with its docks and sea walls. It was indeed beautiful. One eats in a type of patio to the side of the sea wall, all shaded by big trees. By the way, the service was slow, the portions small and the prices high. Keah had "pargo rojo," fish, cocoanut pie; I had "langostinos a la plancha." On the opposite side of the fort to the south is the bay with La Popa Hill and convent above and to the left. There are cannons, sight holes through the walls and all was well preserved.

THE FORT OF SAN FELIPE DE BARAJAS

After lunch we set out for the most famous fort of all—San Felipe de Barajas.

El Fuerte de San Felipe de Barajas and Don Blas de Lezo

The fort is located on the hill of St. Lazarus to the southwest of the old city. It is 41 meters high and was built between 1639 and 1657. There are tunnels constructed below the fort for warehouses, barracks and communications. The fort was taken in 1697 by the Baron de Pointis, but not by Admiral Vernon in 1740. A legend: its mortar contains the blood of fighting bulls. At first it was small when Pointis took it, and only in 1762 to 1769 was it enlarged to the size of today (with the lateral batteries), probably because of Vernon's attack in 1740. Final construction ended with more than 50 cannons, cisterns, barracks, etc. (Curran's note: "I must admit this place must have been the type Walt Disney thought of when designing "Pirates of the Carribbean.")

The idea of fortifying the hill only came after Drake had sacked the city in 1586. The original plans were done by a Dutch engineer; the Low Countries at that time were still under the dominion of Spain via the Hapsburgs and the Holy Roman Empire. Then the fort was "just" a "Plaza de armas, aljibe de raciones, habitación para el castellano, cuartel, hospital, cuatro garitas esquineras y torre de homenaje." This was during the reign of Spanish King Felipe IV. (The name of the fort, "Las Barajas", may be from the name of the home town of the governor of Cartagena at the time.) It had only 14 cannons.

Pointis took the fort and from it cannonaded the old city of Cartagena in 1697. He opened a hole in the old city wall, took Gethsemani Plaza and the city capitulated to him. This of course caused a big debate: either level the fort so it could not be used against the city again or build it bigger so as to not capitulate again. So this was when the Spaniards began to "add on" the subterranean galleries.

DON BLAS DE LEZO.

He was a Basque born in 1689. He lost one leg, one eye, and one arm in the battles of Gibraltar, Tolón and Barcelona. In 1740 spies of Felipe found out about Vernon's plan for attacking Cartagena, so the governor of Cartagena requested Blas de Lezo's fleet to defend the city.

In 1741 the English Vernon arrived with 210 ships, 2070 cannons and 15,000 soldiers (he was the half-brother of George Washington). The Spanish battle defense was interesting: the first line of defense was Bocachica; the second line was Castillo Grande and Manzanillo; the third line was Boquerón; the fourth line was la Popa (which was taken by Vernon) and the fifth line was San Felipe. A combination of Spanish courage in battle, and dysentery, malaria and smallpox defeated the English.

Corner Guardhouse, San Felipe

Massive Lateral Side Construction, San Felipe

We walked the entire fortress of San Felipe: all levels including the tunnels. The view from the fortress of Cartagena below is impressive, but windy. One feels the power and atmosphere of the age from the top of the fort. One "sour" note: it seems that half the tourists urinate in the "garitas" or guardhouses.

One tourist publication stated that Spain spent "69 million ounces of gold" for the entire system of fortifications of Cartagena. When you actually count the number of forts, it seems possible.

MORE FORTIFICATIONS: THE BOAT TO BOCACHICA

Queen Elizabeth II Steamship in Cartagena Harbor

We hired a small tourist boat for the ride. The boat was very simple, made of wood and the "captain" is an old Negro. We passed the docks and the market, watching boats unloading fruit and vegetables; the impression once again was that poverty abounded in this place. In the harbor there were sailboats carrying wood up the coast and larger ships that go out to San Andrés and Providencia islands in the Caribbean a couple of hundred miles east of Nicarágua. Then we saw the luxury liner the Queen Elizabeth II, at that time the largest passenger ship in the world, steaming into Cartagena harbor.

We passed by several forts in the bay that were destroyed (and rebuilt for tourism) throughout those centuries of pirates, corsairs and British and French attacks on Cartagena for its gold. Our destination to the far western end of the bay was Boca Chica which today is a tiny fishermen's town and was extremely poor. There is a strait between two forts and the sea beyond. We heard two different versions of the Boca Chica strait: one that it was closed by a sandbar in the 17th century, the second that it was closed intentionally by the Spaniards to protect the city. The Caribbean side of the city to the east and north of old Cartagena is protected by shallow beaches and reefs thus no ships could come close and there was no need for fortification on that side. Boca Chica is on the west end of the bay.

Outside View, Fuerte de Boca Chica

Fuerte de San Fernando and Boat

At Boca Chica we first saw the fort of San Fernando, 1753-1759; before it was San Luis, almost destroyed by De Pointis in 1697 and then destroyed by Vernon in 1741. It had two batteries called Del Rey and De la Reina, was circular with a moat to protect itself from attack by land from Tierrabomba. Mines were also placed on that side. It was replete with vaults, tunnels and parapets. There were corner turrets and turrets along the walls, much like a medieval castle. The windows were tiny slits, larger on the inside with the idea that a man with a rifle could shoot yet be a small target from the outside. The fort opposite San Fernando was San José on the other side of the strait. It had a huge battery of cannons "a flor del água," at sea level. We counted twenty-one cannons.

After the "serious stuff" we swam in the ocean. Here it was beautiful, a delicious emerald green ocean, as opposed to the slightly muddy water at the beach on Boca Grande. But there were "esmeros" or sea urchins so one had to be careful. Since it is a tourist area, locals offered fried fish. The population is black. There were large cocoanut trees and huts with thatched roofs. We walked about a kilometer to another nearby beach with fresh and delicious water. Then we watched the Queen Elizabeth II leave the harbor.

THE LAST OF THE FORTIFICATIONS: "LAS BODEGAS" ("THE DUNGEONS")

The Fort of "Las Bodegas," Cartagena

On a separate outing we followed the fortified wall on the east side of old Cartagena and the batteries of Santo Domingo and Santa Clara to the part they call the "Bóvedas." Each "bóveda" with its arch is occupied today by a touristy arts and crafts store. One such place had an interesting tavern decorated totally with bullfight motifs; there were posters from Spain and Colombia which depicted bullfights and famous toreadors. But what caught one's attention were the real bulls' heads decorating the walls.

The "Bóvedas" were built from 1789 to 1796, the last of the fortifications by Spain in Cartagena. It was used as an army barracks ("cuartel"), then a warehouse, then a prison during and after the wars of independence. There is a small fort at the very end, aptly called the "Tenaza" or "Tweezers." Note: one of Colombia's great colonial heroes Antonio Nariño was imprisoned for a time in one of the forts prior to Independence.

At this point we had indeed we had seen the major military sites of Cartagena de Indias.

RESTING FROM THE FORTS

Back in town there was a furious run to cash travelers' checks in the Bank of Canada followed by a delicious chop suey of "langostinos y arroz con camarones" at Mee Wah's, and this followed by delicious coconut ice cream across the street. For kicks we walked up to the Hotel Caribe, 5 stars, of the Intercontinental chain and with a daily tariff of 485 pesos per person. It took five minutes to lose a few bucks in nickels in the casino "tragamonedas," well named (money swallowers!)

The next day Keah was under the weather so we had a day of rest at Boca Grande. There was breakfast in an open air café and we watched pelicans diving for fish. There were fruit vendors of pineapple, Keah got her fresh coconut, and Mark got a sunburn. We rewarded ourselves once again with a lunch of eggrolls and rice with chicken at Mee Wah's. That afternoon there was a tremendous windstorm along the beach.

On March 30, 1975, our last Day in Cartagena, we went to the old city to San Pedro Claver for Easter Sunday Mass; it was very, very hot and humid with little breeze. I noted the large church was not at all crowded at the mid-morning mass. I am more than ever convinced that Holy Week religiosity consists in the parade of saints in their elegant wrappings on Good Friday. On that day we saw the Colombian tourists out in droves. Today it was the poor people again. To be noted: Holy Week throughout Latin America is known as vacation time and especially beach time! In Mexico it used to be Acapulco, in Brazil it may be any beach or maybe Ouro Preto; here it is Santa Marta or Cartagena on the coast. Good Friday is no doubt the highlight of Holy Week with its suffering, penance and sadness. The Resurrection on Easter Sunday seemed almost an afterthought, but Boca Grande beaches were jammed. And thus we ended our day.

PART V. EPILOGUE TO COLOMBIA: LA ISLA SAN ANDRÉS, MICROCOSM OF THE CARIBBEAN

The next day we were up early with a last look at the beach and then off to Cartagena airport and its open air restaurant on the second floor. Aero Condor was only about forty minutes late this time, but we had a rough Electra flight to Barranquilla. Then there was a four hour wait for the plane coming from Cali-Medellín-Bogotá (the big jet) which had been held up by fog. We had a smooth flight out to San Andrés Island, beautiful from the air, and one could see the coral reefs and the brilliant blue water with shades of turquoise and green—just what we had planned for the end of the trip.

I divide this narrative in two parts for a couple of reasons: in one sense San Andrés truly is representative of the entire colonial and national periods in the Caribbean and the story is worth telling. The second reason is that the island with all its beauty served us as a well-deserved rest and respite from the serious travel, tourism and yes research on the mainland. So here are both stories.

THE HISTORY OF SAN ANDRÉS—MICROCOSM OF THE CARIBBEAN

San Andrés is a coral island 400 miles north of the Colombian mainland, 120 miles east of Nicarágua, and 250 miles southeast of Jamaica in the Caribbean Ocean. It is eight miles long and 1-2 miles wide. The island is level with one hill 150 meters high, and reefs to the north and east. It possesses coral beaches, clear water, palm trees and many cays. It takes the name "The Sea of Seven Colors" by none less than President Teddy Roosevelt at the beginning of the 20th century.

The culture of the island is a combination of English, Spanish and French; English, Spanish and Patois (a dialect of French) are spoken. The architecture of the buildings is basically English, the religion Baptist.

San Andrés was discovered by Christopher Columbus on his third trip to the New World and named on that saint's day. It appears on the Spanish maritime map since 1527. But at that time it held little interest for Spain.

It was utilized by the Dutch and English corsairs as a point of departure to attack the ships of the Spanish Flotilla. For example, a Dutchman called Blauvelt did commerce with the Moskito Indians of today's Nicaragua, thus the name Bluefields in that country.

In 1629 a corsair ship from Bermuda made contact with San Andrés and gave notice of this to England. The colonists of the Massachusetts Bay Colony then founded a new company to explore the islands of San Andrés and Providencia. Their motives were to cultivate tobacco and to attack Spanish commerce.

1631-1635. English and Dutch colonists arrived. Holland tried to buy the island.

1635. They began the importation of black slaves for farming along with a small number of Algonquin Indians from New England. The project failed because the Indians could not survive the tropical climate and the forced labor in the tropics. Much of the tobacco that was raised was sold to Dutch corsairs.

Then the first colonists from San Andrés and Providencia were sent to British Honduras

In 1640 there was a serious threat to Spanish commerce between Cartagena de Indias, Puerto Bello in Panama and Veracruz on the east coast of Mexico, therefore a Spanish fleet of twelve warships arrived from Cartagena and took the island. Spain took many prisoners, sent the men to Spain and the women back to England. The black slaves remained as property of the Spaniards. But Spain never colonized the island.

In 1670 the Englishman Henry Morgan took the islands again for England and used them as a base to sack Panama (there is a legend of his treasure hidden in a cave in San Andrés,)

1690-1780: There is little activity in the islands; they are uninhabited for seventy years.

1780: There is renewed immigration of a few English families to San Andrés.

1789: As a result of a war in Europe between England and Spain there is a treaty that dictates: Jamaica and British Honduras go to the English; Nicaragua and San Andrés and Providencia go to Spain.

The English colonists who had lived on the island asked the governor of Cartagena to allow them to stay, swearing fealty to the King of Spain, converting to Catholicism and vowing to stop commerce with Jamaica. The islands were declared "minor ports" of Spain.

They had as their first governor an Irish Catholic O'Neil who wanted to increase immigration from people from Jamaica to the island; some 1200 persons arrived, half of them slaves, and the cultivation of cotton was begun. But the real commerce of the island was the contraband of English products to the coast of the Caribbean. There were thirty Spanish soldiers on the island, no Catholic priest, and therefore the people did not become Catholic and continued speaking English.

1806. Captain John Bligh (of "Mutiny on the Bounty" fame) occupied the island for England for two months. O'Neil governed until 1810 and his death. A French corsair, Luis Aury, and some Haitians occupied the islands and remained until 1821, thus bringing a French flavor to the islands.

With the Independence of the "Gran Colombia," Colombia received jurisdiction of the islands by default. It sent a governor, a Mr. Escalón, who became seasick on the journey and never returned to the island.

1820-1850: This was the age of the cultivation of very high quality cotton which was sold to the English and American mills. The only contact by Colombia was a mail boat once a month.

1853: The slaves on the island were freed. One of the results was the change from the cultivation of cotton to that of cocoanuts and an increase in commerce with the U.S. Between 1870 and 1900 San Andrés provided one half of the cocoanut importation to the U.S.

1900: Baptist Missionaries from the U.S. arrived; it was an era of prosperity but with the prohibition of tobacco and alcohol.

1903: The creation of Panamá stimulated the desire of many people on San Andrés to separate from Colombia and become a "protectorate" of the U.S., but the majority voted to remain a part of Colombia.

1930: By now there is less commerce of cocoanuts and more dependence on Colombia (there is fishing only on Providencia, all other food must come from terra firme). At this time there was the imposition of Colombian culture meaning Catholic schools and churches, and many people began to protest. The government of Colombia ceded many liberties and today the island lives from tourism.

1980: A free zone of commerce is declared; there is construction of hotels, gambling is permitted, and the level of life is actually higher than that in Colombia. Colombian culture is generally preserved, but tourism affects everything.

1980: The new government of Nicaragua and the Sandinistas begin a lawsuit against Colombia and want the island for the "New Nicaragua."

So at that time the destiny of the island was once more put in doubt, but it remains in Colombia's hands.

TOURISM, R AND R AND THE END OF THE COLOMBIAN ODYSSEY

San Andrés for Keah and me was truly R and R after the sometimes grueling travel and "research" on mainland Colombia.

Our stay was initiated by a bit of a hassle at the airport. We made the mistake while in the customs line of engaging in conversation with some long haired, hippy types from the U.S. So the customs folks pulled us aside and minutely searched very bit of our luggage. The hassle continued by what we would learn to be a gouging by the taxi driver. But we were rewarded at our modest hotel, the Tiuna," with a sixth floor room with an incredible view facing the ocean.

"The Sea of Seven Colors," "El Mar de 7 Colores," Isla San Andrés

The island sea is called "El Mar de Siete Colores" ("The Sea of Seven Colors") and the moniker is no exaggeration. By the way, an important book by the Colombian Germán Arciniegas on Latin American Civilization uses a similar name: "Latinoamérica: el Continente de Siete Colores." Not before or since have we seen such water, bar none! There were I guess what one could describe as seven shades of gorgeous water out from the white coral beach of the main island with several cays in front. I wrote, "I am sure no place else in the Caribbean matches it." What did I know?

We had most of our meals at the "Fonda Antioqueña" down the beach from the hotel, a modest restaurant open to the sea with reasonable prices and pretty good food (but not to be compared to Mee Wah's). All food on the island is imported from the mainland, and curiously enough there is no fishing at San Andrés. So prices are higher as can be expected and the quality of food is not as good. The "Fonda" is located near the principal dock and its beach and is also the restaurant nearest to the sea. It was rustic in style with benches and tables of wood, posters with "Antioqueña" scenes and a thatch roof.

Palm Trees on the Beach of San Andrés

A long beach runs to the side of the restaurant and from there you can have a motor boat ride out to the cays. Johnny Cay is the best known, about 1-2 kilometers from San Andrés. It for us was the most perfectly romantic island we could imagine, very small with the whitest of coral sand; the sand is light in weight and does not burn your feet even in tropical sun. There are dozens of tall cocoanut trees along the beach. The best of course is the water itself and the reefs beyond; the water seems to vary in color (depending what is below it or if there is sun or not), always a blue, but varying from an almost transparent to a brilliant sky blue, to an aquamarine blue. One sees the seven shades during the boat ride between the main island and the cay (and from the balcony of our hotel room). The water temperature was cool, fresh, but not the slightest bit cold. We rented "máscaras" and fins and swam for hours around the reefs that surround the island. This was a first time for the farmer boy in the Caribbean and a unique experience, different from Keah's experiences at Destin in Florida. It definitely was a "honeymoon" atmosphere. For me it was the first time to see tropical fish, experience snorkeling in such a pretty place, as good as anything I had seen including the Cousteau documentaries. When snorkeling, the depths were bright and clear, not at all dark. One could see rocks, different types of coral and fish of many colors, in groups of three to the hundreds; some black and small, some in brilliant blue or gold, some white and oval with grey borders and a blue and yellow tail (I did not know their names then and certainly do not recall now). Some larger ones, perhaps the size of large Bass, and highly colored seemed to be feeding on tiny animals in the cracks in the rocks, Parrot Fish I surmise now.

So it was one of the most interesting bits of tourism in my life up to that time. Incredible for a land lubber from Kansas! What of course made it better was that Keah truly loves this, so it was a joint adventure. We got home from Johnny Cay extremely tired and with sunburns in spite of massive amounts of oil, but ready to go back. This was followed by dinner at the "Fonda" with a beautiful sunset seen through the outline of the coconut palms.

Author's note: as I read these notes from thirty-five years ago, once again I am struck by the innocence and naiveté of the old "gringo." They seem childish in their pleasure and innocence. Then I think: indeed! What's wrong with that? After all, it was my first experience in the Caribbean and with snorkeling. In today's world of instant pleasure and electronics, I'll still choose the adventures in Colombia before the stuff hit the fan—guerrilla warfare and the drug cartels of the 1980s and 1990s.

We would in future years go on to snorkel off the Yucatán, including a stay at the Hotel Presidente in Cozumel and extensive snorkeling along the Mayan Riviera. And the water, beaches, and tropical fish I am sure more than matched San Andrés. But the latter was indeed a second honeymoon in many ways and the reader I hope can sense a bit of our enthusiasm. A note on the times: our modest hotel and sixth floor room at the Tiuma was a "splurge" costing ten dollars a night!

Moto-Taxi, San Andrés

We rented a "moto" or motorcycle-like contraption to tour the island. It was a real hybrid: a seat welded to two small motorbikes, one of course on either side. The jaunt took two hours and we saw the main island, the airport, the residential side of the island and the west side which is nowhere as pretty as the east side with the coral beaches. The former has no sand and the shore consists entirely of sharp, volcanic rock and its sea is blue but lacking the shades and nuances of the other side. At the south end of the island there is no protective reef so one sees only open sea, huge crashing waves and a "hoyo soplador" or "blow hole" as the main attraction. On the east side one passed through the small seaside town of San Luis with its small wooden houses and island architecture. And we saw the thousands of cocoanut trees.

The following day we went once again to Johnny Cay for the snorkeling. Breakfast was at a small bakery along the beach of the main island where we talked at length with the pretty black girl who served us. On the island they speak English or Spanish but "patois" is the main language, a sort of "pidgin English" with French. To my ear it sounded strange but fascinating; the sound seemed "sing song," light and pretty. It was interesting that on San Andrés I spoke more Spanish than at Cartagena, and it seemed easier to understand than the coastal "brand." I wondered if this was because of the people from Antioquia at the restaurant?

The second day's snorkeling was different. The waves were much stronger, but we were more accustomed to the equipment and handled it all right. But there was a definite current in the water so one had to conserve energy. You can allow the waves to carry you and actually float right along with the fish, kind of using your fins as a rudder. I did see a Jackfish go after another, a new experience. We were just as impressed as before with the sand, the beach and the water. It was different in that the bottom was pure white with coral in the colors of white, red, purple and green. And there were deep parts with coral-like "fingers," like a fan of rock. (The sidewalks in San Andrés are made of coral and you can see the patterns on them that we saw below water.) Again, there was an incredible variety of fish: some white ones, one I think is a Hogshead and a huge one that was the same color as the coral, sliding along the bottom; when it stopped you could scarcely tell it was there. However under all the shelves at the edge of the beaches, the sand was full of sea urchins "with horrible spines." We were warned to be careful and we were. They say the spines can go through the rubber of the dive fins. The current was strong, but if you went in up the beach it would carry you down a way to get out. I ended up believing that this was one of the greatest sports ever! Now I appreciate Jacques Cousteau more. Keah is almost in a state of ecstasy; she is in her element!

On Saturday, April 5, we began our last day on the island.

Mark and Keah on the Beach, "The Aquarium Key," "El Acuario," San Andrés

Mark J. Curran

Breakfast again at the bakery, then a trip to a different key, "the aquarium"("el acuario") by motor launch where we saw a spectacular reef and once again a huge variety of fish. It was different from Johnny Cay in that the current was not so strong, the water was shallow and you could almost but not quite stand on the bottom. From there you could spot one or two more cays in the distance.

After the snorkeling and boat ride back from the cay, we returned for lunch at the "Fonda" and our last view of the Caribbean from that view on the 6th floor. A quick taxi ride to the airport followed.

Aero Condor was on time! On the final trip home we passed over Jamaica and Cuba to Miami. Unlike two or three times in Colombia, there were no problems at customs and an easy return flight to Phoenix.

POSTCRIPT

What an incredible trip! Now in 1986 as I write this, I'm ready to repeat it all. But much has changed in Latin America and in Colombia, and we are no longer in touch with Jim Emery. As mentioned earlier, his father Lorentz was killed in a head-on collision with a bus on the Bogotá-Girardot road. His mother has developed heart trouble and we do not know her exact whereabouts, but only know she had to leave Colombia. John and Jim started an export-import company that did wonderfully well in the 1970s, to the point that the international import-export division of Coca-Cola made an offer to buy them out. Offer rejected. Jim I think is now married to a Colombian girl. We do not know about Linda Buller.

As I said in the brief introduction, this was not simply tourism. I was on sabbatical leave in the spring of 1975 from Arizona State University. The university got two for one: from December to our leaving for Colombia in March I wrote a small monograph which would eventually have great success in Brazil and bring one of its best moments. "Jorge Amado e a Literatura de Cordel" was published in Salvador da Bahia in 1981 and enabled me to be a part of the "Celebration of Fifty Years of Literature of Jorge Amado" in Salvador.

But in those short but intense months in Colombia I accomplished something that would not have to do with publication but which would be much more important in the classroom: documenting the Spanish Colonial Heritage of Colombia as well as the heady days of the War of Independence of Spanish America from Spain. Colombia lived up to its reputation in both. But there was a sad irony: in the late 1970s and the 1980s Colombia was embroiled once again in guerrilla warfare, this time the state versus the Marxist oriented "guerrillas" in the countryside and the "llanos." And shortly thereafter the drug cartel became powerful in the country. I could not honestly encourage my upper division Spanish students to travel to Colombia at that time, so I did not use the material in the classroom as much as I would have liked, that is, with two exceptions. The first was one of my favorite lectures on the Spanish treasure fleet and its route to and from the Americas. There I utilized all the terrific photos and information from Cartagena de Indias. The second, an excuse to show the incredible "Mar de Siete Colores" and San Andrés Isla, was a lecture on San Andrés as a microcosm of history and happenings in the Caribbean during the days of the colony. And, once again, the reason for this book is to write of what I was not able to share in the classroom.

Some months ago I read that a tourist can still go the the Hostería Ucuenguá and the Hacienda Suescún in Boyacá State, but accompanied by a military jeep with a machine gun on top. So it is a bit different than flagging down the old "cucaracha" or local bus in our day. Así sea.

ABOUT THE AUTHOR

Mark Curran is a retired professor from Arizona State University where he worked from 1968 to 2011. He taught Spanish and Brazilian Portuguese languages and their respective cultures. He researched Brazil's folk-popular literature, "A Literatura de Cordel," and has published twenty-five scholarly articles and eleven books in Brazil, Spain, and the United States on the subject. "The Farm" published in 2010 was a change of pace to the auto-biographical, recollections of growing up on a family farm in central Kansas in the 1940s and 1950s. "Coming of Age with the Jesuits" chronicles seven years in Jesuit college and graduate school and his first forays to Latin America. "Adventures of a "gringo" Researcher in Brazil in the 1960s" tells of one year of dissertation research in that country. And now, "A Trip to Colombia—Highlights of Its Spanish Colonial Culture" tells of travel and research in that country in 1975 in preparation for his specialty in Spanish at ASU: Spanish American Civilization.

Books Published:

A Literatura de Cordel, Brazil, 1973
Jorge Amado e a Literatura de Cordel, Brazil, 1981
A Presença de Rodolfo Coelho Cavalcante e a Moderna Literatura de Cordel, Brazil, 1987
La Literatura de Cordel—Antología Bilingüe—Español y Portugués, Spain, 1990
Cuíca de Santo Amaro—Poeta-Repórter da Bahia, Brazil, 1991
História do Brasil em Cordel, Brazil, 1998
Cuíca de Santo Amaro—Controvérsia em Cordel, Brazil, 2000
Brazil's Folk-Popular Poetry—"A Literatura de Cordel"—A Bilingual Anthology in English and Portuguese, USA, 2010
The Farm, Growing up in Abilene, Kansas, in the 1940s and 1950s, USA, 2010
Retrato do Brasil em Cordel, Brazil, 2011
Coming of Age with the Jesuits, 2012
Adventures of a "Gringo" Researcher in Brazil in the 1960s, 2012
Peripécias de um Pesquisador "Gringo" no Brasil nos Anos 1960, 2012
A Trip to Colombia—Highlights of Its Spanish Colonial Heritage. 2013

Curran makes his home in Mesa, Arizona, and spends part of the year in Colorado. He is married to Keah Runshang Curran, and they have one daughter, Kathleen, who lives in Flagstaff, Arizona, and makes documentary films. Her film "Greening the Revolution" was shown most recently at the Sonoma Film Festival in 2012.
Email: profmark@asu.edu
Web page: www.currancordelconnection.com